PENGUIN BOOKS
CONTEMPORARY INDIA

Satish Deshpande studied economics at the Jawaharlal Nehru University,
Delhi, and the Centre for Development Studies, Thiruvananthapuram, before
going on to study sociology at the University of California, Santa Cruz. He
has taught at the University of Hyderabad and is currently a researcher at the
Institute of Economic Growth, Delhi. His interests include the socio-cultural
aspects of economic phenomena; caste and class inequalities in relation to
social policy; spatial dynamics in contemporary society; and the history and
politics of the social sciences in India.

CONTEMPORARY INDIA

A Sociological View

Satish Deshpande

PENGUIN BOOKS

Penguin Books India (P) Ltd., 11 Community Centre, Panchsheel Park, New Delhi 110 017, India
Penguin Books Ltd., 80 Strand, London WC2R 0RL, UK
Penguin Group Inc., 375 Hudson Street, New York, NY 10014, USA
Penguin Books Australia Ltd., 250 Camberwell Road, Camberwell, Victoria 3124, Australia
Penguin Books Canada Ltd., 10 Alcorn Avenue, Suite 300, Toronto, Ontario M4V 3B2, Canada
Penguin Books (NZ) Ltd., Cnr Rosedale & Airborne Roads, Albany, Auckland, New Zealand
Penguin Books (South Africa) (Pty) Ltd, 24 Sturdee Avenue, Rosebank 2196, PO Box 9, Parklands 2121,
South Africa

First published in Viking by Penguin Books India 2003
Published in Penguin Books 2004

Copyright © Satish Deshpande 2003

Typeset in *Aldine* by Mantra Virtual Services, New Delhi
Printed at Chaman Offset, Delhi

For my parents
Ushabai
(née Prabhavati Gurunathrao Kulkarni)
and
Nageshrao Sheshgirirao Deshpande

Contents

Preface

Like people, disciplines sometimes enjoy—or suffer—reputations that they no longer deserve. While this may have worked to the advantage of some disciplines, it has clearly been a liability for Indian sociology and a constant provocation to Indian sociologists. Written partly in response to such provocation, this book was meant to contribute towards the collective task of reviving interest in the discipline. It is specially encouraging, therefore, that readers have responded well enough to justify a paperback edition.

It is, of course, much too early to comment on its substantive failures and successes, but paperback readers are perhaps entitled to some additional help in 'placing' this book. It is easier to say what it is not. This book is not an *introductory* text in the usual sense, although it aims to attract potential practitioners and tries not to presuppose too much fore-knowledge of sociology and social anthropology. It is not a *representative* text, in that it does not seek to portray the 'state of the art' or the current preoccupations of Indian sociology. There are only brief engagements with the works of past or present sociologists and citations have been kept to a minimum—this is not, therefore, a *scholarly* work addressed only to other scholars. Finally, this book does not showcase the successes of the discipline—in fact, it harps on absences, inadequacies and lost opportunities.

I ask that *Contemporary India* be judged not by the negatives mentioned above, but by the seriousness of its engagement with Indian sociology as a whole. This book tries to show *what is at stake* in doing sociology. It presents one vision of what the discipline *could become*. Above all, it tries to demonstrate that all of us have a stake in what sociology does become, and that every thinking Indian stands to gain or lose from its successes and failures. It is addressed, therefore, to all those who help shape the reputations of disciplines—students; scholars from other disciplines; and those who, though not professional academics themselves, have an ongoing relationship with the world of scholarship, such as journalists, writers, bureaucrats, activists, and so on. And it is also addressed to other sociologists in so far as it offers an idiosyncratic but self-critical representation of the discipline designed to stimulate interest in its agendas. Fellow practitioners may disagree with this version, but I hope they will agree on the importance of finding better ways to do what this book has tried to do.

Delhi, January 2004   *Satish Deshpande*

Acknowledgements

Although it is written primarily for the non-specialist reader, this book draws on ideas and arguments culled from my academic writings over the past decade. I am grateful to the following journals/books and their editors and publishers for having published my work in the first instance:

'Imagined Economies: Styles of Nation Building in Twentieth Century India', in *Journal of Arts and Ideas*, Special Issue on *Careers of Modernity*, Nos. 25-26, December 1993, pp. 5-35.

'From Development to Adjustment: Economic Ideologies, the Middle Class and Fifty Years of Independence,' *Review of Development and Change*, v.2, n.2 Jun-Dec 1997, pp. 294-318.

'After Culture: Renewed Agendas for the Political Economy of India', *Cultural Dynamics* (Sage, London), v.10, n.2, 1998, pp.147-169.

'Hegemonic Spatial Strategies: The Nation-Space and Hindu Communalism in Twentieth Century India', in Partha Chatterjee and Pradeep Jeganathan (ed.), *Subaltern Studies XI: Community, Gender and Violence: Essays on the Subaltern Condition*, Permanent Black and Ravi Dayal Publishers, 2000, Delhi. (Previously published in *Public Culture Journal*, v.10, n.2, Winter 1998, pp. 249-83.)

'The Spatiality of Community: Evaluating the Impact of Globalization on Regional Identities' in Surinder S. Jodhka (ed.), *Community and Identity: Interrogating Contemporary Discourses on India*, Sage Publications, 2001, New Delhi.

'Disciplinary Predicaments: Sociology and Anthropology in Postcolonial India', in *Inter-Asia Cultural Studies*, v.2, n.2, November 2001, pp. 247-260.

'Modernization', in Veena Das (ed.), *The Oxford India Companion to Sociology and Social Anthropology*, Oxford University Press, New Delhi, in press.

'Caste Inequality and Indian Sociology: Notes on Questions of Disciplinary Location', in Maitrayee Chaudhuri (ed), *Recasting Indian Sociology: The Changing Contours of the Discipline*, Orient Longman, New Delhi, in press.

'Confronting Caste Inequality: What sociologists must do to reorient social policy', in S.M. Dahiwale (ed.), *Understanding Indian Society: Perspectives From Below*, forthcoming.

If this book finds favour with the general reader for whom it is written, much of the credit must go to Kamini Mahadevan, my editor at Penguin. She initiated this project, and it was her tenacity of purpose that kept it in good health in spite of major delays. But for her copious queries and cautions I would never have been provoked to make the extensive revisions that have had a decisive impact on its final form. I am specially grateful to Kamini and to Kalpana Joshi for accommodating last minute requests despite the inconvenience they must have caused.

My current institutional home, the Institute of Economic Growth, Delhi, has provided a congenial working environment, and I thank my colleagues Aradhya Bhardwaj, T.N. Madan, Nandini Sundar and specially Patricia Uberoi for support and succour over the years. Amita Baviskar and Anindita Chakravarti commented on drafts of Chapter 1, and I thank them both.

I owe a very special debt of gratitude to all my students at the University of Hyderabad, where I taught for nearly five years. It was they who first forced me to think like a sociologist, and more importantly, allowed me to think of myself as one. I also thank the students in my undergraduate course on 'Contemporary India' at the University of Chicago in the Spring of 2001, where most of these chapters were first tried out; their enthusiastic response gave me the confidence to press ahead.

I give thanks to all the friends, comrades and fellow-travellers who have helped me along on the journey towards this book, or the larger voyage of which it is a part: Arjun Appadurai, Ronaldo Balderrama, Sushmita Banerji, Dilip Basu, Aditya Bhattacharjea, Bharat Bhushan, Partha Chatterjee, Maitrayee Chaudhuri, Jim Clifford, Kushal Deb, Vivek Dhareshwar, Anjan Ghosh, Gopal Guru, Kathy Hattori, Keerti Jayaram, Pradeep Jeganathan, Surinder Jodhka, Preetha Kannan, R. Kannan, Sanjay Kumar, Kancha Ilaiah, Harsh Mander, Sebastian Mathew, Rama Melkote, Nivedita Menon, R.Nagaraj, Ratna Naidu, Janaki Nair, Aditya Nigam, Tejaswini Niranjana, Sanjay Palshikar, Rashmi Pant, Sujata Patel, Madhava Prasad, Ashish Rajadhyaksha, Arvind Rajagopal, Nitya Ramakrishnan, N. Raghunathan, Rammanohar Reddy, Sharmila Rege, Aruna Roy, Menaka Roy, Satish Saberwal, Arti Sawhney, David Scott, Meera Shah, Mihir Shah, R. Srivatsan, Marita Sturken, Jim Tharu, Susie Tharu, Carol Upadhya, D. Vasantha and Yogendra Yadav.

This book is dedicated to my parents who had higher hopes for their eldest son, but have learnt to live with the limitations but also the rewards of a life of the mind. The subject of this book, 'contemporary India', was built by their generation and I hope they can see something of what mine has inherited from it.

Finally, I must thank (if that is the word) my son Apoorv, the person most affected by this book, who has already developed a distaste for sociology at age nine; and my wife Mary, the person who has affected this book the most – so much more than just this book would be unthinkable without her.

CHAPTER ONE

Squinting at Society

There are very few jokes about sociologists, as Peter Berger confesses in the opening sentence of his famous *Invitation to Sociology*. As a sociologist, I have always regretted this fact, specially since there are plenty of jokes about our exalted cousins, the economists, and even our more modest siblings in psychology and anthropology have got their share. If forms of humour are one indicator of what matters to society, sociologists and sociology clearly do not.

Though it cannot soothe our injured egos, there happens to be a good reason for the unimpressive public image of our discipline. Other disciplines have the advantage of being perceived as obviously complex subjects requiring specialized knowledge—economics is a good example. But this perception also extends to seemingly less complex subjects that are distanced from everyday life, like exotic cultures or the history of our own or other societies. Sociology is unique among the social sciences for the extent to which its subject matter appears to overlap with the content of everyday life. Everybody is involved in social relationships and institutions; everyone has first-hand experience of social values and norms. Small wonder, then, that sociology fails to inspire awe and is often equated with common sense.

There is nothing specially tragic about this fate: it is shared, more or less, by all disciplines unable to promise access to a well-paid job or to social prestige. But it is indeed ironic—in fact, doubly so—that sociology of all disciplines should be confused with common sense.

The first irony is in the pejorative intent of this equation, which implies that common sense is something simple and self-evident. This is a big mistake, for common sense is really quite a profound and powerful phenomenon. In ordinary language, the phrase usually refers to knowledge or skills acquired 'naturally', i.e, *without being taught*. This may be true in the physical world, where there are some skills that are at least partly untaught or unteachable—like riding a bicycle, for example. But there are no untaught skills in the social world, where society teaches us everything we know, except that, sometimes, it also erases the signs of its teaching. It is precisely this kind of social knowledge—the kind that we are taught to regard as untaught—that sociologists refer to as 'common sense'. Common sense is a vitally important social institution because it supplies the cement that holds up the social structure. That is why the term has a special status in sociology, being used as an abbreviation for a whole range of shared, socially inculcated values, attitudes and habits of thought with which we make sense of our world. (To remind the reader of this special usage, I am converting the phrase into a single word.)

Commonsense is pre-judice in the strict sense—it is 'always already' in place and hard at work long before we make any conscious judgements. It pre-organizes our perceptions in such a way that a large part of the social world is taken for granted and allowed to sink like an iceberg below the surface of our consciousness, leaving only a small part for our explicit attention. Normal social life would be impossible if we and the others whom we interact with did not share a common set of assumptions about the world. That is why interacting with those who don't have commonsense—small children or mental patients, for example—is often stressful, though it can also be quite refreshing.

In their essence, these ideas about commonsense are far from new and quite respectable—'from good family', as we say in India. Three branches of the family tree are particularly relevant because they provide a sense of the different ways in which the notion of commonsense (or something like it) has been considered important in sociology.

One line of descent can be traced back to the German philosopher of phenomenology, Edmund Husserl (1859-1938), and those who brought his ideas into sociology, specially in the US: the underrated theorist, Alfred Schütz, who earned his living as an insurance company executive in New York; the Chicago philosopher, George Herbert Mead, widely influential through his lectures, though all his books were published posthumously; Mead's student, Herbert Blumer who taught sociology at Berkeley (and in his younger days played football for the Chicago Bears); and, more recently, the immensely popular academic writers, Peter Berger and Thomas Luckmann.

Practised under various labels—phenomenological sociology, symbolic interactionism, ethnomethodology—this perspective highlights the fact that the social world, a human construct, has infinite possible meanings which cannot be exhaustively described by the rational methods of natural science. Human actions and communication are based on a shared set of 'background understandings' which are never, and can never be, fully spelt out.[1] We interact by exchanging symbols that convey much more than their literal meaning; human communication is inevitably 'indexical' in that it necessarily depends on what remains unsaid, just like a pointing finger (the index finger, as it is called) always refers to something beyond itself. Thus, phenomenological sociology approaches commonsense with utmost respect, seeing it as an immensely powerful toolkit for encoding and decoding meaning that everyone acquires unknowingly.

Another branch of its intellectual family tree links commonsense to the Italian Marxist thinker and revolutionary, Antonio Gramsci (1891-1937), who was also perhaps the first to use the term in this particular sense. Journalist, theorist of the factory councils movement, cultural critic, general secretary of the Italian Communist Party, and Member of Parliament, Gramsci spent the last decade of his life in

Mussolini's fascist prisons where his already fragile health was irrevocably destroyed; he died at the age of forty-six in a Rome clinic, six days after his jail term expired. Much of Gramsci's intellectual legacy is contained in the thirty-three 'Prison Notebooks' smuggled out of his room during the funeral arrangements and sent to Moscow by diplomatic bag. Gramsci is a key figure in Marxist thought because he makes the difficult transition from the world of the founders of Marxism—whose faith in the imminent collapse of capitalism seemed justified by the trend of historical events (like the European revolutions of 1848, the Russian Revolution of 1917, or the Great Depression of the 1920s and 1930s)—to the world we inhabit, where such faith can no longer be sustained.

The effects of this transition can be seen in Gramsci's notion of commonsense, which he describes as the 'philosophy of the non-philosophers', the uncritically adopted conception of the world that ordinary people inherit from their socio-cultural environment. Embodied in popular language, religion and folklore, commonsense is a chaotic collection of contradictory beliefs and attitudes; but the prevailing power structure imposes a partial coherence on it by highlighting some elements and marginalizing others. Thus modified, it serves to bind the moral conduct of individuals to the norms of the social groups they belong to, and bends these norms themselves towards the dominant ideology. In this way, it helps to legitimize the power structure by securing the passive (and occasionally the active) consent of the broad mass of people. But because of its contradictory contents, the coherence imposed upon commonsense is always vulnerable to subversive reformulation. Gramsci's notion of commonsense rescues the Marxist theory of ideology from its earlier reliance on a crude mixture of coercion and 'false consciousness'. Since contemporary capitalism cannot be overthrown by swift armed insurrections, ideology becomes the decisive battleground on which a protracted 'war of position' must be fought to recast commonsense and give it a new, radical coherence.

A third branch of the family tree connects commonsense to the contemporary French anthropologist and sociologist, Pierre Bourdieu (born 1930, died 23 January 2002). Influenced by both phenomenology and Marxism, Bourdieu's early ethnographic work in the Kabylia region of Algeria in the 1950s and 1960s was intended to be 'fieldwork in philosophy', part of an attempt to construct a 'theory of practice'. Bourdieu's version of commonsense is his notion of the 'doxa', or that portion of our world that seems so self-evident that it is silently accepted—because it 'goes without saying', and because we are not aware that things could possibly be otherwise. The doxa is the sphere of socially invisible unanimity that precludes both ortho-doxy and hetero-doxy: unlike them, it refuses to recognize the presence of other opinions and hence the possibility of dispute.

The concept of doxa is part of Bourdieu's attempt to solve the age-old agency-structure riddle in social theory—how to explain the co-presence of both free will and institutional constraint in the actions of ordinary people? He suggests that the doxa helps reconcile structure and agency by prompting people to freely choose what they are in fact forced to choose; the self-evident sense of 'proper limits' that it instils allows the individual to 'mis-recognize' objective structural constraints as active subjective choices. While doxic commonsense helps maintain order in pre-capitalist, 'traditional' societies with 'enchanted' social relations and a 'good faith' economy, its grip weakens during the crisis-ridden transition to the disenchanted world of modern capitalism and the 'callous cash' economy.

These three views of commonsense—from phenomenology (how is it that we know so much more than we can ever explain?); Marxist social theory (how do people consent to a social order that treats them unjustly?); and ethnography (how do people's subjective choices come to mesh so well with their objective constraints?)—expose the power and scope of this vastly underrated social institution. Indeed, it is an institution so central to social theory that sociology could well be described as the critique of commonsense. My favourite among the many possible definitions of the discipline, this description also highlights the second irony inherent in the popular perception of sociology as commonsense on stilts.

For to think thus is to confuse a science with the object of its inquiry, which is a bit like mistaking a geologist for a rock. But such analogies are misleading because they conceal the complexity of the relationship between commonsense and sociology. Geologists need not worry about rocks shaping their minds, whereas sociologists must constantly worry about commonsense doing precisely that. And there is no simple or permanent solution for this anxiety.

It is easy to forget, given its connotations in everyday language, that commonsense is not simply a fancy term for the simple-minded naïvetes of other people. No one is immune: indeed, one could say that to live in society is to live in commonsense. It is said that Archimedes offered to lift the earth if given a big enough lever and a place to stand. But there is no Archimedian vantage point—no 'place to stand'—outside the world of commonsense from where we can practise a pure and scientific sociology. As social scientists now recognize, the previous search for 'value neutrality' is a mirage, because the social sciences are themselves a product of the society they wish to analyse, and they cannot but be influenced by the environment they inhabit. So, rather than think in terms of an unattainable ideal—value neutrality—it is better to accept the potential for bias and try to describe its possible sources as carefully and completely as possible. Unlike the traditional approach where the social scientist retreats behind a professional mask of faceless anonymity, this approach requires the foregrounding of all the aspects of research that used to be considered 'backstage' features: the researcher's personal identity and background, the conditions in which the research was carried out, and so on. At the same time, attempts to ensure a bias-free methodology are also intensified—but they are now contextualized by the realization that our efforts to transcend commonsense are always partial and provisional.

The main advantage that commonsense offers to sociologists is that it is not a single seamless monolith that engulfs all of society in the same way at the same time. Every epoch, social group or specific context produces its own sense of what is self-evidently right or wrong, what goes without saying. This all-important fact—that commonsense is not the same in all times and places, or for all people—provides a wedge with which we can prise open its closed circuits of meaning. We can study the effects of commonsense by switching perspectives: by looking at the world from the viewpoint of differently placed persons or groups, or even by imagining a world different from the one we inhabit, much as writers and artists do. It is thus possible to analyse one kind of commonsense by consciously locating oneself within another kind, using the contrast to trace the outlines of what would otherwise be very difficult to see. But this is not easy and it certainly does not come naturally—it demands constant, disciplined effort, something like the *riyaaz* required of classical musicians. 'Sociology' is the name, among other things, of precisely this kind of *discipline*.

There is a second foothold that commonsense provides for those wishing to scale its otherwise smooth and slippery walls. This is the fact that it is always implicated in power relations. The most effective and durable forms of domination in society are ultimately based on commonsense; conversely, a significant portion of popular commonsense leans in the direction of power. It is important to recognize, however, that the mutually supportive relations between power and commonsense are neither inevitable nor permanent—they are context-driven. More importantly, commonsense also contains much that is hostile to the dominant order and provides the potential for resistance and rebellion. Nevertheless, we can take advantage of the power-commonsense correlation by using the former to unveil the latter. Just as Anil Kapoor's character in the 1980s hit film *Mr India* is normally invisible but shows up in red light, commonsense can be made visible in the light of power relations.

Positioning sociology as a critique of commonsense exposes us to the risk that we will begin to think of commonsense as something that is necessarily wrong or false, something always in need of correction. This is a temptation to be resisted. The point about commonsense is that it represents our *unexamined* and often *unconscious* beliefs and opinions. What is objectionable here is not necessarily the content of beliefs and opinions, but that they are arrived at unthinkingly, through habit, ignorance or oversight. The goal of critique is to convert 'pre-judice' into 'post-judice', so to speak. *After* we subject commonsense to rational scrutiny, we may find that it contains values and norms we cherish and wish to defend; or we may find that it harbours deceptions that distort our perspective on the world; or we may find both to be true simultaneously, or even that it is difficult to decipher what is going on. Sociology may or may not be helpful in this 'after' state, but its main mandate is to help us break out of the 'before' state of unawareness. The Greek philosophers believed that an unexamined life was an uncivilized one; sociology helps us to identify and interrogate the unexamined aspects of our lives.

If 'commonsense' is an abbreviation for the transparent pane of unexamined prejudices through which we normally view the world, 'sociology' is an abbreviation for the abnormal gaze that tries to focus on both this pane as well as the world beyond it. Figuratively speaking, therefore, sociologists need to cultivate a sort of double vision, a squint. To split a phrase that describes a squint-eyed person in colloquial 'Bihari'—among the richest of the many hybrid languages invented in contemporary India—good sociologists must always strive not only to 'look London' but also to 'see Paris'.

This book invites you to practise 'squinting' at Indian society. It surveys the careers of ideas and institutions like modernity, the nation, caste, class and globalization in the half-century since Independence. At the same time, it tries to make visible and subject to scrutiny the commonsense that surrounds not only these ideas and institutions but also past and present efforts to study them. It invokes 'the sociological imagination' to illuminate the sites where personal biographies intersect with a larger social history. It hopes, above all, to instil a sense of wary respect for all that seems self-evident, and to whet the appetite for self-questioning. In short, this book explains why it is cool to be cross-eyed, and shows you how to 'see double'.

The peculiar predicament of Indian sociology

Thus far we have spoken of sociology only in its global, or more accurately, its universal-Western avatar. But as with all the cultural sciences, this universalism is never quite complete, and the discipline has a somewhat different look in non-Western and specially ex-colonial contexts like India. It is important to address these differences for they influence the stance of the discipline and impart a particular flavour to its commonsense.

The dictionary defines a predicament as a 'difficult, perplexing or trying situation', and there are three special aspects to the one that afflicts Indian sociology. They are closely related and together shape the distinctive profile of the discipline: first, the ambivalent image that sociology inherits from the colonial era; second, the disciplinary consequences of the twinning of sociology and social anthropology that is peculiar to India; and third, the persistent anxiety about the Indian-ness (or lack thereof) of Indian sociology.

In the course of its re-establishment as a discipline in independent India, sociology seems to have fallen between economics and history. Both these latter disciplines were gifted enormous energy and momentum by the nationalist movement. Economics—commensurate with its global status as the dominant social science of the capitalist era—was seen as the discipline providing the cutting edge to the case against imperialism. In keeping with the requirements of modern nationalism, history was given the responsibility of (re)constructing the past of the emergent nation. Most important, both disciplines could easily carry over their agendas into the post-independence era. Economics, of course, became the mainstay of Nehruvian socialism and the premier language in which the modern nation was articulated. History took up the task of writing a retroactive biography of the nation, rescuing various regions, classes and movements from the condescensions of colonialist historiography.

In sharp contrast, sociology seems to have inherited a profoundly ambiguous and disabling self-identity. This was a direct consequence of the fact that it lacked a distinct presence in colonial India, being largely subsumed under social anthropology and Indology. These two met with divergent responses from educated Indians, and this split carried over into the post-independence reputation of sociology. On the one hand, the nationalist elite approved of orientalist Indology in so far as it documented classical Indian/Hindu achievements in literature, philosophy and the arts, and enthusiastically celebrated them. Indeed, Indian-Hindu religio-spiritual traditions and culture were the crucial fulcrum on which nationalist ideology leveraged itself. Asserting India's cultural-spiritual superiority enabled the acceptance of undeniable Western economic-material superiority and the forging of a nationalist agenda for fusing the best of both worlds.[2] Social anthropology, on the other hand, met with hostility and resentment because it was perceived as deliberately highlighting the 'barbarity' of Indian culture and traditions.

This antipathy is vividly evoked by M.N. Srinivas, the most famous of Indian sociologists. Recalling the days of his youth when 'anthropology, unlike economics, political science or history, was unpopular with educated natives in colonial countries', Srinivas mentions that in India this was partly due to the notoriety of Katherine Mayo's book *Mother India*. (First published in 1927, this sensational account of sexual depravities, child marriage, infanticide, untouchability and other horrors was bitterly attacked by nationalists for presenting a distorted view of Indian society catering to Western stereotypes; Gandhi described it as 'a drain inspector's report'.) Srinivas describes how, in August 1943, he was chased out of a middle-class club in Vijaywada

> by a fat walking-stick-wielding lawyer who thought I was planning to do a Katherine Mayo on the august culture of the Telugus. I was asking questions about caste, kinship, festivals, fasts and fairs when the angry lawyer lunged at me and said, 'get out, we have no customs'. (Srinivas 1992:133.)

The contrast in the public response to social anthropologists and economists is instructive. Although the latter documented the wretched living conditions of the Indian masses, they and their discipline could nevertheless be framed as patriotic and anti-imperialist, for India's poverty could be attributed to British rule and turned into an argument for independence. Our 'customs and manners', however, could not be so easily disowned. Often cited by colonialists as proof that India did not deserve independence, they were an embarrassment for nationalists trying to speak the modernist language of their opponents.

Unlike the transformation of the economy or polity, where the past could be left behind without much soul-searching because it was thought to be neither integral to national identity nor worth salvaging for its own sake, 'the passing of traditional society' and culture was apt to be viewed with mixed feelings.[3] Tradition was an area of considerable ambivalence because, on the one hand, it contained the ideological wellsprings of social solidarity, cultural distinctiveness and hence nationalism; but, on the other hand, it was also the source of atavistic 'social evils' and other signs of backwardness that a modernist, forward-looking nation could not afford to dwell upon. In sum, social anthropology found it difficult to join the chorus of other disciplines singing songs of redemption in newly independent India; burdened with an equivocal past, the discipline needed radical rethinking.

The all-important context for such a rethinking was that of a new nation embarking on a massive state-led programme of 'nation building' with economic development as its dominant motif. Understandably, the concrete forms taken by the nation-building project had an enormous impact on the academic-intellectual field. Disciplinary identities and agendas were recast in response to direct or indirect state sponsorship and the prevailing ideological climate. Although the science and technology-related disciplines were the main beneficiaries, the social sciences also profited from the huge expansion of the research and higher education establishment in India during the 1950s and '60s. In the planned and unplanned gerrymandering of disciplinary boundaries that this process inevitably involved, Indian sociology found itself at a disadvantage.

Some part of this disadvantage was perhaps due to its union with social anthropology. Indian social anthropologists have generally refused to abide by the conventional distinction between anthropology as the study of 'primitive' or traditional societies and sociology as the study of 'complex' or modern societies. There is a lot to be said in favour of this refusal: the archaic separation is no longer practised; the two disciplines are closely related and overlap significantly; and, finally, both types of society that each allegedly specializes in coexist in a country like India. Although a merger of two disciplines implies that the product can claim the names of either or both of its parents, in India the label of sociology has been preferred over social anthropology. This preference may have been motivated mainly by the desire to downplay the embarrassing association with colonialist anthropology, and perhaps also the need to distance the discipline from physical anthropology (including palaeontology and anthropometry) which had a strong presence in India.

Whatever the motivation, it cannot be denied that the composite discipline of Indian 'sociology' is heavily tilted towards anthropology, and would be known by that name elsewhere. When they go abroad, Indian sociologists are treated as anthropologists and invariably visit departments of anthropology rather than sociology. The overwhelming majority of the scholars influential in the profession, both Indians and specially Westerners, have been trained as anthropologists. The most intensively-studied areas have been caste, kinship, religion, village and tribe, rather than the class structure, cities, markets, industrial relations, or the media. In terms of methods, too, anthropological specialities such as participant observation and informant-based field work have been very prominent, while survey research and quantitative analysis have rarely been influential.[4]

The trajectory of Indian sociology may not have been very different even if its internal composition had been otherwise. The new national priorities which prompted the post-independence restructuring of academia did, after all, re-order the hierarchy of disciplines. At the global level too, the reasons which made the latter half of the twentieth century 'the age of economics' could not be wished away. By the same token, other disciplines could not simply erase their pasts and reinvent themselves. My point, therefore, is *not* about disciplinary 'luck'—I am not asking why sociology isn't more like economics. Granting that sociology would receive only a small share of the academic space given to the social sciences, my point is that its anthropological bent may have prevented the discipline from fully occupying even this small space.[5] In the (sociological) areas which could claim a prominent place in the nation-building project, the composite discipline was relatively weak and therefore suffered encroachment from its more assertive neighbours. On the other hand, the (anthropological) subjects where its authority was undisputed often ran counter to the ideological inclinations or the perceived practical needs of the new nation.

Consider, for instance, the vast terrain claimed by that capacious cliché, 'socio-economic'. Because it has a narrow methodological base and is ill at ease with 'macro' analyses, Indian sociology has ceded more ground to economics here than it need have. Indeed, recent demands for a fuller analysis of the socio-cultural aspects of economic institutions have come more from economics than sociology. While it is easy to understand why predominantly economic themes like poverty (for example) have spawned an immense academic and para-academic literature, it is puzzling that sociology has remained so aloof from this mainstream.[6] It has been left to economists and political scientists (and to organizations like the UNDP or the World Bank) to underline the importance of social capital, gender inequalities, caste- or community-based networks, and other such social phenomena in understanding poverty or responses to it. The 'bad luck' of the discipline cannot be the only reason why sociologists have not been centrally involved in any major national initiative during the four decades that separate the Community Development Programme of the 1950s from the Mandal controversy of the 1990s.

The third peculiarity that marks the predicament of Indian sociology also stems from its merger with anthropology, though in a different way. This is the recurring anxiety about the *Indian-ness* of

Indian anthropology-alias-sociology: is it Indian enough? Can it—should it—be made more Indian?

Anxiety may seem an oddly extravagant word, but I wish to highlight precisely the extra concern that the social sciences provoke in non-Western settings. The natural sciences have always believed that they are unaffected by their historical-cultural location, although some doubts may have crept in recently. The social sciences are on the whole less confident on this score, but there are significant differences among them. Economics and history, for example, seem to carry the burden of cultural/historical specificity lightly, though for very different reasons. Given its past, it is not surprising that these concerns should weigh most heavily on anthropology. Here, issues like cultural specificity, colonial power and racial domination were not merely part of an external context, they were integral to the theoretical warp and methodological weft of the discipline. Acknowledging the distorting effect of Western-colonial contexts did not require Indian academics to dump disciplines like history or political economy. Practitioners could see that it was possible to keep the baby and get rid of the bathwater by practising nationalist historiography or development economics. Things were different with anthropology: to state the contrast crudely, it was much more difficult to decide what brown people should do with a discipline that was basically designed by white people to study non-white people.

The spectrum of possible responses was bounded at one end by a position that denied any link between colonialism and anthropology, and saw no problem in continuing with business as usual in the post-colonial era. At the other end was the belief that a fundamentally orientalist discipline like anthropology had no post-colonial future—to borrow the old feminist epigram, it would be as useful to independent India as a bicycle to a fish. The variety of actual responses that eventually unfolded cannot be described in simple terms; they certainly did not take the shape of a golden mean. However, common to most of them was an undercurrent of anxiety about the Indian-ness of the discipline, an anxiety born of the fact that the very idea of an

Indian anthropology runs against the historical grain of the discipline.

A famous founding precept of the discipline says that the anthropologist studies cultures *other than* her/his own native culture. But we also know that, despite the abstract neutrality of this principle, the practice of anthropology has been profoundly asymmetrical, consisting almost entirely of Western researchers studying non-Western subjects. Consequently, both the Western-ness of the anthropologist and the 'non-Western-ness' of the 'other' cultures he/she studied were well entrenched in the commonsense of the discipline as self-evident norms. Against this background, the non-Western anthropologist stood out as an oddity—all the more so when studying her own culture, because the 'study-only-strangers' rule was also violated. And for reasons that seem obvious but need more careful scrutiny, non-Western anthropologists (unlike their Western counterparts) have almost always ended up studying their own societies. It has rarely been possible for them to study the West, or even non-Western cultures other than their own; and the few existing efforts of this sort have not had any significant impact on the mainstream of the discipline, although some distant rumblings have been heard recently.

Thus, the anxiety about Indian-ness may have begun as a largely unselfconscious and often muddled response to this messy history. Seen as oddities but wanting to be taken seriously, the early Indian anthropologists may have been somewhat uneasy about the tacit tension between their national-cultural and their professional identities. But if this was true when the post-colonial era began around 1950, it is no longer so today, when disciplinary norms and practices appear to have changed considerably. Any lingering self-doubt in Indian sociology-anthropology today is not fuelled by unease about studying one's own society. If anything, the shoe is on the other foot. Heightened awareness of the discipline's past has raised doubts about the intended or unintended effects of Western scholarship on India. Apart from colonial contamination, there has also been a more generalized fear that alien theories or theorists might not be able to produce a sufficiently accurate or authentic account of Indian culture and society. It is these vaguely defined but strongly felt misgivings that have prompted repeated calls for a truly indigenous sociology.

There are several interesting paradoxes and peculiarities associated with this phenomenon. For instance, foreign scholars have been among the most insistent advocates of an indigenized sociology based on native concepts. There is also the historical irony that much of the intellectual ammunition used by nationalists of every variety—including specially the historical and Indological work on the past glories of Indian civilization and culture—has been provided by Western scholarship. Finally, the all-important fact is that despite its emotive-intuitive appeal, it has proved very difficult to even define, leave alone create, an indigenous science of society.

It is easy to demonstrate that most indigenist positions usually boil down to an understandable but intellectually incoherent nostalgia. But there are other, quite coherent, reasons for focusing attention on the national-regional domicile of disciplines. When we simply refer (as we often do) to 'sociology', 'anthropology' and so on, we are assuming that these proper nouns denote universal entities that belong equally to all humans without regard to nationality, race, class, gender or any of the myriad other particularities which divide humankind. This is true in an important albeit rather abstract sense, and it is imperative that we keep renewing our faith in this assumption. However, at a more concrete and experiential level, we also know that this abstract universality is more fiction than fact. Although they often claim a grandiose vagrancy—that they belong to no place and all places simultaneously—the modern academic disciplines do have a fixed address. They do not relate to all places or to all kinds of people in the same way, and the reverse is equally true.

This is not just a question of differences but of *inequalities*. Like the rest of the world, the academy, too, is full of glaring disparities in access and influence. The dominance of the West over the rest in the field of knowledge production has been one of the taken-for-granted aspects of academics in our time. Western libraries are better stocked with materials on non-Western countries than libraries in these countries themselves; scholars based in the West have access to more material and non-material resources, are more 'visible' and have a greater impact on global disciplines than their counterparts located in non-Western countries, and so on. India has been a partial exception in some disciplines and contexts, and it is also true that things have been changing rapidly. Nevertheless, it needs to be reiterated that globalization has not diminished these disparities—it has only displaced and complicated them. At the same time, we also need to remind ourselves that these complex inequalities are not only international—they are just as integral to intranational institutions, relationships and processes.

The net result is that we can no longer afford to be naïve about the universalist claims of academic disciplines, least of all in cases like anthropology or sociology. It is now not enough to speak of 'sociology', or even 'Indian sociology,' without qualification. Further questions are inevitable today even though they may not have easy answers: is Indian sociology simply the sociology *of* India? Who or what is it *for?* Does it matter who it is practised *by*, and where its theories and methods come *from?* Though they may not be equally relevant in all contexts, these are not trivial questions nor are they due merely to misplaced national chauvinism. They are a product of the fact that the self-understanding of the social sciences has been transformed by recent work uncovering the systematic synergy between structures of power and institutions of knowledge.

The realization that 'Indian sociology' is a disparate field marked by inequalities and asymmetries along several criss-crossing axes demands from us a double vigilance. We have to be alert to the possibility that the persuasive power of a theorist, the content of a theory, or the career of a concept may be affected by where they are located on the global grid of unequal power relations that regulates knowledge production. But we also have to be on guard against reductive formulae that insist on a fixed relationship between location and content. Every location has inherent possibilities and constraints, but they do not take effect automatically: they must be scrupulously investigated in each case. In the final analysis, the effects of location must be demonstrated, not assumed.

'You are here': A route map for this book

The concluding section of this introduction provides a sketch map of the route through Indian society and sociology that is taken up in the following chapters. But first, in keeping with the emphasis on self-reflexivity in this book, I must provide its readers with some indication of where its author is coming from.

Like others of its kind, this book too has been shaped by a variety of factors: the author's areas of interest, competence, and ignorance; disciplinary trends that encourage or discourage particular fields; publishers' assessments of the commercial viability of different themes or formats; the inevitable mix of accidents for which no one can be credited or blamed, and so on. Other things being equal, authors generally tend to overstate the part played by their own intentions and plans in this process. At the end of a long and arduous journey, we are inclined to claim that the destination reached is precisely the one aimed for in the beginning. This is usually only partially true, but there is an understandable and perhaps also necessary tendency to underplay its partialness. After all, the author's job is not merely to impose coherence on chaos but also to provoke and—ideally—to persuade.

My main aim has been to write a book that would advertise the attractions of sociology—its distinctive stance towards the world, and the special insights it offers. My intended audience, therefore, has been a non-specialist one, including the general reader wanting to think beyond commonsense, academics from neighbouring disciplines, and students across the social sciences and humanities. But after the book was done, I found that I had all along been addressing myself as well. Perhaps it is a sign of the times that, even more than others, it is we sociologists who need to rediscover the attractions of our discipline.

The overall theme, specific subjects and mode of presentation in this book are, as far as I can determine, products of three sets of causal factors. The first is my 'naturalized' rather than native citizenship in Indian sociology; the second is my formative experience as a teacher; and the third involves the contingent historical events of the last decade or so.

My repeated insistence on a singular disciplinary perspective may seem odd, specially in view of the fact that I have never had any formal training in the specific subject area of this book, namely the sociology of India. I did my bachelor's and master's degrees in economics, and was halfway through a doctoral programme at an Indian research institute when I wandered off to an American university and into the discipline of sociology, in which I earned a second master's and a doctoral degree. Due to institutional encouragement and force of circumstance, most foreign (and specially 'Third World') social science students in Western universities end up writing theses on their native countries. Out of a perverse resistance to such prodding, I insisted on a 'local' topic and wrote a dissertation on the centrality of an 'extra-economic' phenomenon like racism to California's clearly capitalist agriculture. Although I hardly realized it at the time, this also meant that I did not study any Indian sociology. Why, then, do I harp on the specificity of the discipline? Such disciplinary monogamy appears particularly incongruous today when inter-, multi-, trans-, and even anti-disciplinary perspectives are much in vogue. And surely it is carrying things too far to insist on differentiating sociology even from social anthropology?

In keeping the focus firmly on sociology, my motive is not to deify disciplines or to re-erect barricades between them. In fact, the following chapters will often trespass, quite casually and without fuss, on to territory claimed by economics, anthropology, political science or history. My point is different: the inclusive enthusiasm of labels like 'inter-disciplinary' makes us forget that systematic scholarship also requires ruthless exclusion. This is a necessity, not a failing; we are able to study some subjects or master some methods only by refusing to deal with others. Descriptions like interdisciplinary or multidisciplinary may give us a vague sense of the something 'extra' that is being included, but they remain silent on the exclusions that must inevitably accompany the inclusions. As a result, we are no longer aware of what we don't know, and risk ignoring lopsided patterns of disciplinary development. Indian sociology is an excellent example: the claim that it is both social anthropology as well as sociology has served to divert attention from the uneven growth of its two components. Because the discipline has been less than ambidextrous, I dwell on the distinctive identity of sociology only to favour the weaker hand.

This book is about certain subjects and perspectives that I think have been underemphasized, and 'sociology' happens to be the most convenient label under which they can be grouped, particularly since it also helps to focus attention on the processes responsible for this relative neglect. But beyond this, the name does not really matter; what matters is the awareness of what is being excluded or included, and why. The best known authors and the most influential books associated with 'Indian sociology' have generally focused on the important subjects of caste, kinship, religion, village society or tribal cultures, and they have done so, by and large, from an anthropological perspective. Of these themes, all except caste are absent from this book. Even among the more sociology-oriented themes, this book does not cover key areas like agrarian and industrial relations, demographic trends or the media. These omissions do not imply—and I cannot emphasize this enough—that these subjects are in any way less important or deserving of study. They are the price paid for focusing, from a 'macro' or society-wide perspective, on five ideas, institutions and processes—modernity, nationhood, inequality, caste, and globalization. The emphasis throughout is on examining that which has seemed (or still seems) self-evident, not because everything self-evident is necessarily false, but because unexamined beliefs need to be converted into self-conscious ones.

This selection of topics and perspective is directly due to my lack of formal training in Indian sociology, and specially to my being forced to teach what I had never been taught. I had been a teacher of economics before, but that was a subject I had been taught; I had also taught sociology in American universities at the doctoral and undergraduate levels, but that did not involve India. Teaching sociology in India, I felt the difference acutely. I felt not just like an outsider—a feeling that the discipline believes to be useful and in fact fosters—but like an impostor. I felt the full weight of a hundred years of sociology on my sagging shoulders every time I walked into the classroom and struggled to 'discipline' my students.

The struggle was initially conducted in the theory courses of the MA programme. Given the logic of the curriculum in Indian universities, this usually means Western sociological theory unencumbered by any social context. On this terrain, I had the advantage for I had specialized in 'theory' and had taught it for some years. On the other hand, my students were put on the defensive by the difficulty of the material and the aura of a foreign degree; perhaps my apparent sincerity also prompted them to be indulgent and they hid their bafflement and exasperation. Emboldened by what I fondly believed to be my success in teaching theory, I ventured to teach 'applied' courses on contemporary society, hoping to impress my students with the usefulness of what they had been taught.

I soon realized, however, that on this terrain my students had the upper hand. My lack of formal training in Indian sociology meant that I did not possess the commonsense of the discipline, and had not internalized its mental reflexes. Nor did I possess the pragmatic ability to choose my battles wisely. In this state, I was very vulnerable to the visceral accounts of lived experience that my students threw at me. Once they persuaded me to look at sociology and at the world through their eyes, I could neither deny nor explain away the serious mismatch between the two. It was like a jigsaw puzzle where the pieces of the right shape have the wrong part of the picture on them. Bewildering and painful, it was also a profoundly provocative experience, and I will always be grateful to my students and my lack of training for this unconventional initiation into Indian sociology.

I believed, quite plausibly, that my initial difficulties were simply the product of ignorance and lack of experience. If only I read more books and read them more intensively, if only I examined my students' examples and arguments more carefully, I would be able to fill the gaps between theory and social experience or at least explain why they need not or could not be filled. This was true to a large extent, and rapid progress was made as my reading broadened and deepened, and as I learnt to sift through individual experiences to separate 'personal troubles' from 'social problems'. But many problems persisted even after several years of teaching and could no longer be explained by individual ignorance alone (which in any case is a permanent state, varying only in degree and direction).

For example, caste was a live and volatile issue on the campus with frequent clashes between Dalit and upper-caste students. But despite the vast literature on this subject in sociology, I could find very little that directly addressed their experience. It was almost as if the caste that sociologists studied and the caste that was part of everyday social experience in the university were two different things. I could analyse caste only by anaesthetizing it in the classroom, 'like a patient etherized upon a table'. Whenever I encountered it in its live and active avatar in events on the campus, I was at a loss. In the same way, marriage was an important and sometimes even a traumatic subject for students, specially the women, many of whose families saw the MA course as a stopgap arrangement while searching for a suitable match. But the sociological literature on kinship, marriage and the family seemed light years away from the kind of strategizing and the pressures and counter-pressures faced by these young women and their families. 'Endogamy' in the real world was a hugely complex, constantly evolving institution that easily outflanked the available academic analyses.

It was not only such issues of immediate experience that sociology did not seem to address adequately, but also larger ones. The bitter anti-Mandal agitations had only just died down when I began teaching, the demolition of the Babri Masjid followed soon after, and communal riots were already an integral part of life in the city. Although I was deeply affected by both events, the former was specially painful professionally. It was hard to accept that a discipline that had studied caste intensively for decades had nothing more to say about Mandal than countless columnists and self-appointed pundits.

No academic discipline should be expected to provide a ready-made manual for living or a guide to current affairs. But why has Indian sociology been unable, by and large, to respond to the unprecedented opportunities it has been presented with in recent times? The last two decades should have belonged to sociologists. They should have belonged to us because, for the first time in the history of independent India, the nation faced a number of 'big' problems that looked and were more social than economic. Secessionist movements in Punjab and Kashmir based on ethnic-religious identity; the Mandal controversy and the intrusion of caste into a supposedly caste-less urban middle-class milieu; the advent of Hindutva and its elevation of the communal divide on to centre stage in the national polity; and the widespread concern about the cultural impact of globalization—all these developments (to name only four) were ideally suited for major interventions by sociology and other non-economics social sciences. But our response has not been equal to the challenge, or at least that is how it seems. I am not sure why or how this has happened, and this book is part of an attempt to think through this predicament.

It would be foolish to believe that Indian sociology can obtain something like the magical 'solution to all problems' promised by the sex-clinic ads scrawled on the walls of Delhi. But I do hope that this book will contribute more to the solutions than to the problems, and that students and teachers of sociology and neighbouring disciplines will find it useful. Most of all, since I was one myself not so long ago, I hope that the 'general reader' will want to know more about the

CHAPTER TWO

Mapping a Distinctive Modernity

Modernity—together with its contrasting twin, tradition—is among the most ubiquitous themes in the commonsense of contemporary India. An intense and contentious aspect of the process of nation formation, the desire to be modern has become so deeply ingrained in our national psyche that its signs and symptoms are visible all around us.

Consider, for instance, the frequency with which the word 'modern' has been used as a name: for a well known journal (the *Modern Review*) published from Calcutta in the early 1900s; for a popular brand of bread made by a public-sector company 'privatized' recently; for an elite school in Delhi; and most significantly, for countless shops and small businesses—tailors, 'hair cutting saloons', dry cleaners, 'variety stores' and so on—in cities and small towns all over the country. (In fact, if there were a contest for guessing the most popular (non-proper noun, English) names for small businesses in India, my money would be on 'modern', 'national' and 'liberty', probably in that order.)

I came across a slogan that could well have been the epigraph for this chapter in another peculiarly Indian place of public culture—the graffiti hand-painted on vehicles, in this case a Delhi bus. 'Unhe bhi to pata chale ki ham bhi *modern* hain', it said—they should realize that we too are modern. The slogan used to be the punchline of a 1980s television ad. More recently, the beauty queens that we are now producing with monotonous regularity have repeatedly informed the world that the essence of Indian womanhood is the blending of tradition with modernity. No Indian needs to be told that this theme has been among the perennial obsessions of our popular cinema across all genres and regions. In the realm of 'high' culture as well, the question—what qualifies as 'modern' and what should be our attitude to it?—has generated intense literary debates in every major Indian language, and in every discipline in the arts, specially painting and dance.

Why does the idea of modernity have such a massive presence in Indian social life? What makes it such a big deal?

Everyone above the age of fifteen will have worked out some version of the commonsense answer to this question. Modernity becomes a big deal because we are desperate to be, and to be acknowledged as, modern; but at the same time, we don't want to be 'too modern', or 'only modern'—we wish to be modern on our own terms, and we are often unsure what these terms are or ought to be.

This isn't a bad answer, and you need read no further if you are satisfied with it. But this book is for people who are not content with commonsense; if you are one of them, and have sometimes wondered *why* the modernity-tradition theme has become the mother of most clichés, do read on.

'Modern': A short social history

The English language inherits the word 'modern' from the ancient Latin, where it has been in use since at least the sixth century of the Christian Era. For the first twelve hundred years or so of its history, the word was used in a generic sense to characterize the *distinctiveness of any contemporary era* in order to distinguish it from past eras. Around the eighteenth century, the word acquired a new and more specific sense that referred to the *unique social system that emerged in Western Europe* between the seventeenth and nineteenth centuries, and the values and institutions associated with this system.[1]

In pre-nineteenth century English usage, 'modern' appears to have been a pejorative term with strong negative connotations, and we are told that 'Shakespeare invariably used the term in this sense' (Black 1966:5). However, as Raymond Williams points out, 'through the nineteenth century and very markedly in the twentieth century there was a strong movement the other way, until *modern* became virtually equivalent to improved or satisfactory or efficient' (Williams 1983:208-9).[2] Although 'modern' still retains its comparative-temporal sense of something close to or part of the present, it is interesting to note that, in the last decades of the twentieth century, this sense has been yielding ground to words like 'contemporary' or to neologisms prefixed by 'post'. Moreover, the word is no longer unequivocally positive in its connotations.

These recent developments in the career of the word point to a complicated and unequal relationship between its two meanings: the generic one has generally been subordinated, whether surreptitiously or openly, to the specific meaning. The consequences of the dominance of the sense connoting Western European modernity can be seen quite clearly when we shift from the relatively static noun—modern—to the more dynamic and processual verb, *modernization*. Modernization entered the English lexicon during the eighteenth century, mainly in references to changes or improvements made to buildings and spelling, at a time when the reversal of the pejorative connotations of the noun-form had already begun. By the twentieth century the word had become increasingly common and was 'normally used to indicate something unquestionably favourable or desirable' (Williams 1983:208-9). This general connotation of a process of *positive change or improvement* (particularly with reference to machinery or technology) was inflected—specially when speaking generally about social institutions or entire societies—by the suggestion of a more pre-determined movement towards the *European Enlightenment model of modernity*.

Unlike other attempts to distinguish a modern present from its pasts, modernity is not content with establishing a merely relativistic difference but claims fundamental superiority. As Arjun Appadurai has put it, European modernity

> both declares and desires universal applicability for itself. What is new about modernity (or about the idea that its newness is a new kind of newness) follows from this duality. Whatever else the project of the Enlightenment may have created, it aspired to create persons who would, after the fact, have wished to have become modern. (Appadurai 1997:1.)

Once claimed, such normative privileges pre-position modernity in a profoundly asymmetrical relationship to all other epochs and cultures.

These claims have, of course, been much more than abstract assertions, having had the status of self-evident truths for most of mainstream social science. Whether in terms of a contrast with the world of *tradition* (another critical keyword of modern times), or in terms of the coherence of its own multifaceted achievements, there is a formidable array of evidence proclaiming the uniqueness of post-Enlightenment Western-European modernity. Some of this evidence is eloquently recounted by Lloyd and Susanne Rudolph:

> '[M]odernity' assumes that local ties and parochial perspectives give way to universal commitments and cosmopolitan attitudes; that the truths of utility, calculation, and science take precedence over those of the emotions, the sacred, and the non-rational; that the individual rather than the group be the primary unit of society and politics; that the associations in which men live and work be based on choice not birth; that mastery rather than fatalism orient their attitude toward the material and human environment; that identity be chosen and achieved, not ascribed and affirmed; that work be separated from family, residence, and community in bureaucratic organizations ... (Rudolph and Rudolph 1967.)

To this long list of the attributes of modernity we must also add the revolutionizing of modes of governance with the emergence of democracy, the modern nation-state and its institutional apparatus;

the advent of new and intensified notions of time; and, at a somewhat different level, the supplanting of God and Nature by Man and Reason as foundational categories, and the consequent penchant for 'metanarratives' (or grand story-lines) of various kinds, most notably those of Progress.

It hardly needs emphasizing that the ideas and institutions of modernity have wielded enormous material and moral power. Like all other social systems, modernity too has been historically and culturally specific; but it is the only social system in human history that has had the technological capability, the social organization and the systemic will-to-power to comprehensively reshape the whole world in its own image. Colonization is only the starkest form of this reshaping, which begins with pre-modern Europe itself, and passes through the de-population and re-settlement of the New World, to the direct or indirect subjugation of the rest of the globe. The mental-moral forms of colonization have been even more profound in their effects: whatever be our attitude towards it, modernity has shaped to an extraordinary degree the ideological frameworks we inhabit, the intellectual tools we use and the values that we hold dear.

This overgeneral sketch needs to be qualified and complicated in a number of (sometimes contradictory) ways. Despite the remarkably convergent forces and processes it has unleashed across the globe, modernity has hardly been a single unified entity. Indeed, it is only at the highest level of abstraction that one can speak of something simply called 'modernity'. Not only have disparate, even incompatible perspectives been produced within its ambit, but modernity has itself spawned oppositional philosophies of various kinds (such as the romanticism of a Rousseau or the nihilism of a Nietzsche). And though it is true that modernity's attempts to colonize the world have been largely successful, this has usually meant that other cultures or social systems are not simply erased, but are subjected to intense and sustained pressure. Moreover, by the twenty-first century, modernity has legitimized itself in most parts of the world and is more a freely chosen goal than an alien imposition.

Modernity Outside the West

An important aspect of modernity is the fact that it is also the source of the conceptual tools that have been used to understand it. In this sense, therefore, modernity defines our intellectual horizon rather like commonsense—there is no place to stand outside of it. The social sciences as we have known them are themselves products of and responses to modernity, having emerged in the post-Enlightenment era in Western Europe (Hawthorn 1987). The discipline of sociology, in particular, was invented as part of a larger attempt to make sense of this new and historically unprecedented social system. The classical theorists acknowledged as the founders of the discipline—including August Comte, Karl Marx, Emile Durkheim, Max Weber, Herbert Spencer, and Ferdinand Toennies—were all concerned with theorizing the Western European experience of *modernization,* the process of becoming or being made modern.

It should not surprise us that it is only in the 1950s—more than half a century after the institutionalization of disciplines like sociology—that academic interest in modernization extended beyond the West. Until then, non-Western societies were considered to be non-modern by definition, and were studied either by anthropologists interested in 'primitive' cultures or by orientalist scholars investigating the past of once-great civilizations.

But the world changed very rapidly after the end of World War II. The process of decolonization, which coincided with the beginning of the Cold War, gave birth to a 'Third World' consisting of a host of new African and Asian nations who had gained independence between the late 1940s and the 1960s. On the one hand, decolonization released fresh hopes and energies in the new nations across the globe, at a time when boundless faith was being invested in the idea of unlimited material progress based on rational-scientific technologies. But, on the other hand, there was no fundamental change in the socio-political, and specially the economic, inequalities undergirding the world order. The new nations thus became both the repositories of millenarian agendas of change and progress fuelled by domestic aspirations, as well as potential client states where the old and new world powers competed to establish spheres of influence. Added momentum was provided by the almost total hegemony of the US over the Western world.

'Modernization studies' were launched in the early 1950s as part of a vast, largely US-sponsored multidisciplinary academic project with the overall objective of winning the Cold War—both negatively (by preventing the 'slide into communism' of poor Asian, African and Latin American nations), and positively (by providing socially, economically and politically viable routes to stable non-communist growth and development). As part of this enterprise, various US federal government institutions (including the military), leading universities, and private philanthropic foundations (notably the Ford and Rockefeller foundations) financed a historically unprecedented volume of social scientific research on the new nations of the Third World (Myrdal 1970:12-16, Gendzier 1985, sp. Ch.2). Moreover, nationalism and independence also awakened in the middle-class elites of the Third World an intense interest in the development and modernization of their own societies, often translated into state support for research, or at least into willing cooperation with externally sponsored research efforts.[3] Seen against this background, the emergence and popularity of theories of growth, development or modernization seem almost inevitable (Myrdal 1970:8).

Ironically, despite its three-fold division, the world was also being *unified* in a way it had never been before. Although centuries of plunder, trade, warfare, religion, conquest and colonialism had fostered global intercourse of various sorts, the developments of the twentieth century were without precedent. Campaigns to eradicate disease in the early decades of the century created the notion of a global human population collectively at risk, while the Great Depression of the twenties and thirties dramatically illustrated the interdependence of national economies. By the time the fifties came along, the mind-boggling scale of new weapons of mass destruction and the spectacular successes of space exploration had altered human consciousness forever, imbuing it with a powerful sense of a single shared planet.

It was in this historical context—in an intellectual climate where deep divisions coexisted with ideas of commonality, change and convergence—that Western social science first addressed the non-Western world through modernization studies. How, it asked, would—should, could—these clearly non-modern societies become modern?

Although it soon came to be dominated by development economics and allied fields, the thirty year boom (1950s-1970s) in modernization studies affected several disciplines including sociology (specially rural sociology), area studies, political science and social psychology. Sociology played a particularly prominent role both because it provided the most commonly invoked theoretical framework—namely, the highly abstract (hence apparently context-free and cross-culturally portable) taxonomic syntheses of Talcott Parsons—and because of the inevitable importance of rural sociology in studying predominantly rural Third World societies. The major themes taken up by modernization studies included development, the transition from traditional to modern social forms, the aids and obstacles to the emergence of modern political institutions, and the inculcation of (or resistance to) modern values and norms in the individual personality.

Even if we know now that they led to an intellectual dead end, modernization studies did mark a significant moment in the global history of the social sciences. At the very least, their naïve confidence in modernization as a theory of 'the true, the good, and the inevitable'—as Arjun Appadurai (1997:11) has put it—triggered our scepticism and forced us to rethink the vexed relationship between modernity and non-Western societies.

THE SPECIFICITY OF INDIA

While it is, of course, strongly affected by this global background, the history of modernization studies in India is also rather distinctive. Unlike in most other Third World countries, American modernization theory did not dominate the study of social change in India, although it was a prominent and influential presence in the realm of state policy. This difference is due to the combined effect of three factors: the prior involvement with India of other Western scholarly traditions; the presence of a small but relatively well-developed indigenous research establishment; and the hegemonic influence exerted by a long-standing nationalist movement.

As an ancient civilization with a living Great Tradition (rather than a 'decapitated' one, to use Robert Redfield's starkly evocative term[4]), India was no *tabula rasa* for Western scholars. The production of systematic knowledge on Indian society of a recognizably modern kind developed very rapidly from 1760 onward, based on the pioneering work of Orientalist Indologists, colonial administrators and missionaries, as Bernard Cohn has shown (1987:141-171). By the early decades of the twentieth century these varied traditions had already produced a considerable body of works on the arts, sciences and cultural-religious practices of classical Hinduism; the cultural coherence of Indian/Hindu or aboriginal communities; and regional inventories of castes and tribes detailing their 'customs and manners'. To this must be added the later work of Western and Indian scholars trained mainly in the British tradition of social anthropology, as well as some American anthropologists, consisting largely of ethnographic monographs on village, caste or tribal communities.[5]

However, this diverse body of largely anthropological work on India did not show any deep or sustained interest in social *change*, except in the form of inquiries into the decay or degeneration of traditional practices, institutions and communities. With independence, of course, the search for social change became an important item on the agenda of social anthropology in India—so much so, in fact, that some scholars worried that it would eclipse other issues.[6] But even when it did get taken up, this search was conducted largely independently of American modernization theory as such, in keeping, perhaps, with the relative indifference towards this theme in anthropology.[7]

The second and third reasons for the Indian difference have to be viewed together: the social dominance of nationalism in the 1950s, and the existence of institutions that could give intellectual expression to this dominance. In India, as in most of the non-Western world, the themes of modernization, development, growth and progress were part of the much wider canvas of the colonial encounter, particularly since the latter half of the nineteenth century. They were woven into colonialist narratives of the white man's burden and the *mission civilisatrice*—and also into emergent nationalist narratives of the desire for development thwarted by colonial oppression and economic drain. In the heady aftermath of Indian independence, the idea of modernization took on the dimensions of a national mission; it became an integral part of the Nehruvian 'tryst with destiny' that the nation had pledged to keep. While Indian nationalism in itself was hardly an aberration (though older than most others in the Third World), India's colonial inheritance of a viable nucleus of Western-style academic institutions was unusual, possibly even unique. Like other social institutions of the time, Indian universities and research institutes were also eager to participate in the agendas of the nationalist state, and provided another site for the emergence of modernization studies in India, albeit one marked by an ambivalent attitude towards Western scholars and institutions.[8]

Anxiety And Ambivalence

'We may have become weary of the concept of modernization,' writes T.N. Madan (1995:5), 'but the important question is, have we carefully formulated the reasons for this weariness?' Indian sociology does seem to be weary of this theme—not only bored or disenchanted, but also exhausted by it.[9] Why has the conceptual pursuit of modernization been so debilitating?

A DISCREPANT DUALISM AND ITS DISCONTENTS

Some of this weariness may have been caused by the frame of analysis commonly used to understand modernization, namely dualism. The dominant view among students of modern India held that neither tradition nor modernity would be strong enough (at least in the foreseeable future) to completely erase the other. This meant that the search for an adequate summary-description of Indian society was converted into the problem of defining dualism—or characterizing the nature of the relationship between tradition and modernity.

There is nothing exceptional in this, for dualism is the presiding deity in the conceptual pantheon of modernization not just in India but everywhere in the 'non-West' (Banuri 1990:40-3). Consider, for example, one of the most famous vignettes in modernization studies— the story of 'The Grocer and the Chief'—with which David Lerner begins his classic work on *The Passing of Traditional Society* (Lerner 1958:21-28; subsequent quotations in this paragraph are from these pages). Presented as 'the parable of modern Turkey', this story contrasts two main characters who stand for modernity and tradition. The chief (of the village of Balgat, 8 km south of Ankara) is a 'virtuoso of the traditional style'. A prosperous farmer and an imposing personality, he has no unfulfilled ambitions, loves to expound on the values of 'obedience, courage, loyalty', and responds to persistent inquiries about where else he would like to live with a firm 'nowhere'. Balgat's only grocer is described by his interviewer (a Turkish student identified only by the abbreviated name Tosun B.) as an 'unimpressive type' giving 'the impression of a fat shadow', whom the villagers consider to be 'even less than the least farmer'. But the grocer visits Ankara frequently, is fascinated by Hollywood movies, would like to own 'a *real* grocery store' with floor-to-ceiling shelves, and is eager to live in America because it offers 'possibilities to be rich even for the simplest persons'. As if to underline the centrality of this dichotomous model for modernization theory, Alex Inkeles and David Smith present an identical contrast between Ahmadullah, a 'traditional' illiterate farmer from Comilla, and Nuril, a 'modern' metal worker in a Dhaka factory, who enact Lerner's Turkish parable all over again—sixteen years later, in Bangladesh. (Inkeles and Smith 1974:73-83.)

The point of recalling these emblematic figures is not to claim

that they are absent in India—how could they be?—but to highlight
the fact that the *dominant* descriptions of dualism in the Indian literature
are different. Simply put, Indian descriptions of dualism seem
discrepant because they are relatively more sophisticated than those
elsewhere, at least in the early period of modernization studies. The
precociously complex analyses of influential scholars like M.N.
Srinivas minimize the impact of the cruder models of dualism, even
though they are as common in India as elsewhere in the Third World.
On the other hand, this means that the dead end of dualism is reached
sooner in India and more time is wasted in the futile effort to grasp
Indian social reality in terms of the tradition-modernity dichotomy.

The most obvious differences in Indian accounts of dualism have
to do with the social units in which tradition and modernity are located
and their mutual articulation. Thus, tradition and modernity are not
only segregated into two separate personalities as in the Bangladeshi
or Turkish tale, but are also apt to occur, in comparable Indian accounts,
as integral parts of *the same personality*. For example, M.N. Srinivas
mentions meeting the 'driver of a government bulldozer' on his field
village of Rampura in 1952, barely two years after Tosun B. met with
the Turkish grocer and chief on Daniel Lerner's behalf. The bulldozer
driver, a Tamil-speaker from Bangalore, was skilled enough to operate
his machine and also to 'do minor repairs; but he was not only
traditional in his religious beliefs, he had even picked up some black
magic, a knowledge usually confined to small groups'. Srinivas reports
that 'he saw no inconsistency between driving a bulldozer for his
livelihood and indulging in displays of black magic for his pleasure',
the 'two sectors being kept completely "discrete."' (Srinivas
1971a:54 5.)

But if such descriptions are more believable and complex than
the caricatures of crude dualism, they also place the Indian personality
under permanent suspicion of schizophrenia. Here is Srinivas again,
speaking this time of the first generation of his own community, South
Indian Brahmins, who

   took to English education in considerable numbers and

entered the professions and government service at all levels. In the first phase of their Westernization, their professional life was lived in the Western world while their home life continued to be largely traditional. (The term 'cultural schizophrenia' comes to mind, but a caution must be uttered against viewing it as pathological.) (1971a:57)[10]

The theme of the coexistence of 'discrete' sectors in a single person, family or other social group is a common one in the literature on modernization in India, and, indeed, in the conversational anecdotes of everyday life.[11] The dualistic-but-unified personality may be described in a wide range of registers—from pathos through pathology to pride. But whatever the tenor of the description, and regardless of the attitude of the person being described, the describer—specially the professional social scientist—is unable to shake off a sense of incongruity which invariably inflects the description.

Nevertheless, in the Indian literature, the choice between tradition and modernity is rarely presented as a mutually exclusive 'either-or', though it is often seen as a morally charged one. In Lerner's description, tradition has no value whatsoever for the grocer, who wishes only to escape from its parochial constraints; and the chief, though forced to acknowledge the impact of modernity, remains thoroughly immune to it morally. In this parable, 'modern Turkey' is the only transcendent entity capable of subsuming these contrary world views, while in the Indian literature the burden of subsumption is felt by social units all along the scale from the national to the individual.[12]

There is another difference that seems important: the prominence of *Indian* scholars in the social anthropology of India. In India, the Western anthropologist encountered not only natives and 'local counterparts' (brahmin pundits, gyanis or maulavis), but also his/her own '*double*', the native anthropologist with comparable Western training (Burghart 1990; see also Das 1995:34-41). Such an early and sizeable presence of local scholars is quite unusual among

Third World countries, and may well be unique.[13] Whatever the reasons responsible, the crucial question is whether the presence of Indian researchers made any difference to the *descriptions produced*.

Returning to the comparisons between modernization in Lerner's Turkey and Srinivas' India, a striking difference is now visible. Tosun B., the Turkish graduate student whose field notes caught Lerner's attention and helped produce the parable, is himself outside the frame of reference, or, at best, at its edges. By contrast, Srinivas, the anthropologist with an Oxford degree, is never allowed to forget his Indianness, and is constantly being pulled into the frame of the picture he is painting.[14] Perhaps it is this sustained incitement to self-reflexivity that makes Indian accounts of dualism precociously complex. Indian anthropologists are acutely aware that modernization is happening not just 'elsewhere' but in the 'here and now' that they themselves inhabit.

Whatever the truth of their claim to greater sophistication, Indian accounts of dualism cannot escape the limitations of this mode of theorizing. Modernization—even in its minimalist version of an ongoing interaction of some sort between tradition and modernity—proves to be a conceptual dead end because there is, literally, no exit. A modernizing society is always only a modernizing society: it can no longer call itself traditional, and its modernity is never quite the real thing. In a strange twist on the 'allochronism' (Fabian 1983) that anthropology is accused of, the modernization paradigm evacuates the present of such societies, robbing it of its immediacy and constricting its relations with the past and the future into narratives of loss or inadequacy. It is truly remarkable how this motif of a society, a culture, a history, a politics or even a personality permanently in a state of in-between-ness—a double-edged failure—recurs across disciplinary contexts.

For example, in anthropology, the 'developing societies' become (in the words of T.N. Madan) 'deceived societies as they have had their present transformed into a permanent transition', 'an endless pause' (1995:165, 22). In Marxist political economy, (as Mihir Shah puts it in his requiem for the mode of production debate), 'Indian agrarian relations are perhaps destined forever to remaining semi-capitalist' (1985:PE-66). And Ranajit Guha inaugurates the 'Subaltern Studies' initiative with the announcement that the 'central problematic' of historiography is the 'failure of the nation to come into its own' (Guha 1982:7). All the various avatars of this theme—whether in the garb of a search for modernity, democracy, capitalism, or development—are marked by the anxiety of striving for a norm that is unattainable from the very beginning.

THE INTERNAL BIASES OF INDIAN SOCIOLOGY

The internal composition of Indian social anthropology may also have contributed to the impasse in modernization studies. In Indian social anthropology the distinction between sociology and anthropology has been refused at least since Srinivas (that is, since the mid-fifties or so). This is an unexceptionable refusal in so far as the convention of the former studying 'complex' and the latter 'simple' societies could not really be followed in India and is no longer the rule elsewhere either. However, the well-established Indian practice of referring interchangeably to sociology and anthropology hides the fact that the latter is much better developed here than the former. Because the social anthropology of India was heavily oriented towards 'tradition'—that is, towards institutions like caste, tribe, kinship and religion, and towards rural rather than urban society—modernization studies here were also biased in this direction. Had urban sociology, economic sociology, social history or political sociology been better developed, the content of modernization studies may have been more balanced, with the new and emergent getting as much attention as the old and traditional. As it happened, most studies of modernization in India located themselves in the world of tradition and looked out upon modernity from that vantage point, with its attendant strengths and weaknesses. Indian social anthropology failed to cultivate intensively those methods (such as survey research or quantitative techniques) and research areas (like industry, the media or the class structure) of sociology proper which fell outside its usual zone of intersection with anthropology. This, in turn, affected the manner in which the discipline dealt with the question of modernization, particularly since this question privileges a macro perspective, something which anthropology is neither theoretically inclined towards nor methodologically equipped for.

THE CATHOLICITY OF THE CONCEPT

Part of the difficulty that Indian sociology has had with the theme of modernization may be due to the vastness of the term itself. It is pertinent to recall here that modernization was introduced into social theory as a very broad, catch-all concept that was considered 'useful despite its vagueness because it tends to evoke similar associations in contemporary readers' (Bendix 1967:292). As Dean Tipps has written in an important critique:

> The popularity of the notion of modernization must be sought not in its clarity and precision as a vehicle of scholarly communication, but rather in its ability to evoke vague and generalized images which serve to summarize all the various transformations of social life attendant upon the rise of industrialization and the nation-state in the late eighteenth and nineteenth centuries. These images have proved so powerful, indeed, that the existence of some phenomenon usefully termed 'modernization' has gone virtually unchallenged. (Tipps 1973:199.)

This may sound somewhat exaggerated in the Indian context—the momentous and swift transformations taking place here were clearly very real and significant. But the question of whether 'modernization' was a useful conceptual basket into which all these varied changes could be thrown did bother Indian scholars sensitive to the 'messiness' of the process.

The fact that in modernization theory, this process is 'defined in terms of the goals towards which it is moving' (Tipps 1973:204) is particularly problematic not only because the direction of change is difficult to determine, but also because this goal itself involves conflicting ethical-moral values and claims. The sensitive scholar's instinctive distrust of such treacherous terrain is seen in Srinivas' doubts and queries: is all social change to be called modernization? Is modernization the same as Westernization?[15] Similar instances can be found in the work of most scholars, and the very existence of many different viewpoints shows that these doubts are not easily settled.

Problems And Prospects

As already noted, modernization has been an omnibus concept, a sort of summary description of epochal dimensions based on an underlying dichotomy between tradition and modernity. If there ever was a time when such an abstract, generalized dichotomy was conceptually useful, it is surely gone now. All the common uses to which it was put—to indicate a division of global society into different spheres, to refer to a similar division within a given society, or to distinguish between past and present—are no longer viable because, today, there are as many similarities as differences across the divide.

'Most societies today possess the means for the local production of modernity,' as Appadurai and Breckenridge point out, 'thus making even the paradigmatic modernity of the United States and Western Europe (itself not an unproblematic assumption) no more pristine.' (1996:1.) To continue to refer to non-Western or Third World societies as simply 'traditional' is therefore seriously misleading. Similarly, if one were to believe, with Robert Redfield, that '[t]he word "tradition" connotes the act of handing down and what is handed down from one generation to another' and that it therefore 'means both process and product' (quoted in Singer 1975:x), then it is clear that no sharp division can be made between tradition and modernity in the long term. On the one hand, what is modern for one generation will perforce become part of tradition for the next; on the other hand, the product that is passed on cannot possibly exclude the modern. Analytically, it seems futile to think of 'tradition' and 'modernity' as though they were the names of distinct pre-existing objects or fields of some kind; it is more fruitful to think of them as value-laden labels which people wish to attach to particular portions of what they inherit or bequeath. Descriptively, no purpose is served by this contrast after the thorough diffusion and domestication of modernity across every conceivable area of tradition.

However, it would seem that this very ubiquity of modernity has created a new use for 'tradition'—not as a descriptive term, but rather as a 'space-clearing' or 'distinction-creating gesture' (Dhareshwar 1995b:PE108). Tradition of this sort—that is, invoked as a sort of claim-to-difference—is itself a product of modernity, and forms part of the reservoir of resources with which modern adversaries fight each other. Thus, in a very general sense, everything and everyone is modern today, the Taliban as much as Microsoft, velcro and vibhuti as much as dowry and debentures. This does not mean, of course, that everyone and everything is *the same*—just that the traditional-modern axis is unable to tell us anything useful about the very important differences that distinguish contexts, institutions, processes or relationships.

Another angle on the non-viability of the high level of abstraction at which terms like tradition, modernity and modernization have been pitched is offered by recent attempts to re-examine the self-evident unitary status of most objects to which these terms used to be applied. The nation-state is an obvious example: 'fragmentary' perspectives may have their own problems, but it cannot be denied that the taken-for-granted status of entities like 'India' or 'the nation' has suffered serious damage (Pandey 1991, Chatterjee 1994). This break down of its objects of reference also serves to evict the concept of modernization from its high perch.

Contemporary Responses

If 'modernization' has lost its analytical-heuristic value as a summary-description of epochal sweep, this is as much due to the internal collapse of the tradition-modernity dichotomy as to the external attacks by dependency theory and world systems theory. But there are as yet no obvious successors, though terms like 'post-colonial', 'post-modern', and lately, 'globalization' have been hovering in the wings. However, the most noticeable change in Indian social theory today is the marked increase in confidence vis-à-vis the West. (In this, theory seems to have followed social life rather than the other way around, but that is another story.) While such self-assurance was not exactly unknown before, it is probably more widespread and sophisticated, and certainly more ambitious now. Indian scholarship has developed an 'attitude' by the 1990s and is no longer overawed by Western disciplinary dominance. In the wake of such confidence, contemporary responses to the demise of the modernization paradigm seem to take four broad routes.

DOWNSIZING AND AVOIDANCE

The most common response has been to avoid the term—modernization is no longer invoked in the grand theory mode. If it is used at all, the scope of the term has been scaled down, and it seems to be returning to the specific technical sense in which it first entered the English language (e.g., for buildings, machinery and spelling). Since it is only at very high levels of abstraction and generalization that the term has proved a failure, it may still be serviceable in restricted contexts with clear referents, as for example, in the modernization of libraries or irrigation systems. However, this amounts to banishing the term from social theory.

RECLAIMING THE PRESENT

The previous response simply rejects one of the main functions of modernization as a summary-description—a name—for an epoch in which societies previously described as 'traditional' begin to experience rapid change. What gets obscured, however, is that this epoch is a contemporary one, that it constitutes the present of the societies undergoing modernization: the teleological orientation is so strong that descriptions of the journey are overwritten by descriptions of the destination. If modernization studies in general tend to 'evacuate' the present, those within social anthropology are doubly affected because of the discipline's old habit of constructing an 'ethnographic present' in which other cultures are 'distanced in special, almost always past and passing, times' (Clifford 1986:9). It is not surprising, therefore, that some recent initiatives in this discipline (and elsewhere in the human sciences) have concentrated precisely on the recovery and reconceptualization of contemporaneity. Thus, for example, Veena Das undertakes an anthropology of 'critical events' explicitly in order 'to reflect on the nature of contemporaneity and its implications for the writing of ethnography' (Das 1995:4); Geeta Kapur confronts the problem of identifying the 'founding equation between history and subject' that might help define the contemporary moment in cultural practice (Kapur 1991:2805); Madhav Prasad seeks to go 'back to the present' to signal not 'the nation's arrival at some pre-determined telos, but *arrival as such*, arrival in the present as the place from which to find our way forward' (Prasad 1998b:123, emphasis original); and Vivek Dhareshwar asks what it means to be modern if 'our time' is one where the conditions of intelligibility of 'the key words of our cultural and political self-understanding' no longer hold (Dhareshwar 1995:318; 1996). More generally, these and other such attempts are part of an effort to pay rigorous attention to the historicity of the present without allowing this historicity to be hijacked by the teleology of notions like modernization. As D.P. Mukerji (1955:15) reminds us, it is more important to understand 'the thing changing' rather than 'change per se'.

EXPLORING EMERGENT LOCATIONS

As outlined in the previous section, Indian social anthropology has until recently been concerned mainly with tradition and how it copes with modernity. This has meant that modernity has been viewed through the frameworks of tradition and has been looked for in its 'traditional' sites, so to speak. These, of course, are not the only or necessarily the most important ones where it is to be found—indeed, it is one of the hallmarks of the contemporary era that eruptions (or claims) of modernity may take place in the most unexpected locations. For example, the slogan painted on a bus that I mentioned at the beginning of this chapter—'They should realise that we too are modern'—is also the punchline of a mid-1980s television ad for sanitary napkins. It is spoken by a mother as she hands a package of napkins to her daughter (who is returning to her in-laws), the connotation being that the napkins will prove to the 'boy's side' that the girl comes from a 'modern' family. That a television advertisement would deliberately foreground menstruation in this manner can hardly be anticipated by conventional notions of the 'inner/outer' and 'private/ public' domains. Examples of scholarly attempts to explore systematically such unconventional sites where the peculiarities of Indian modernity find expression include recent studies on social aspects of the film-form in India,[16] and new work on the domain of sexuality and its linkages to such varied institutions as the state, the media, the law, and academic disciplines such as demography or anthropology.[17]

COMPARISONS ACROSS THIRD WORLD CONTEXTS

For both obvious and less obvious reasons, the lateral contacts among sociologists of non-Western countries have been few and largely under the auspices of Western institutions. Unfortunately, what Srinivas and Panini said a quarter century ago still remains true, including specially their concluding observation:

> Paradoxical as it may seem, the very need to understand Indian society requires from Indian sociologists a commitment to a

comparative approach in which the problems, processes and institutions of their society are systematically compared with those of neighbouring countries in the first instance, and later with other developing countries. So far such a comparative approach has been conspicuous by its absence. (Srinivas and Panini 1973:48.)

Though some Indian sociologists have indeed worked on other Third World countries (Ramakrishna Mukherjee on Uganda; Satish Saberwal on Kenya and J.P.S. Uberoi on Afghanistan, for example), the impact on the discipline at large has been negligible. Third World countries have always only provided the non-Western empirical grist for Western theoretical mills. As the Brazilian sociologist, Mariza Peirano, points out:

the moment we leave behind the frontiers of the country, what here was a theoretical discussion, almost immediately becomes merely regional ethnography (1991:326).

It is only through this kind of cross-cultural comparative work in Third World contexts that we can move beyond tiresome lamentations of Western intellectual hegemony to a situation where the specificities of Indian, Turkish, Indonesian or Brazilian society can finally refuse to be merely 'local colour' and aspire to be part of 'global theory'.[18]

Beyond Commonsense

The stakes in modernity were raised enormously in non-Western contexts, where the idea of modernization arrived dressed up as a 'secular theory of salvation'.[19] The defining condition of non-Western engagements with modernity was that its ideas and institutions were 'always-already' marked as Western. Given that even the most benign forms of colonization involved an adversarial relationship with the West, this immediately created a tension, a predicament. Modernity was the object of intense desire, at the very least because it promised resources with which the marks of colonial subjugation could be erased and equality claimed with the erstwhile masters. It was also the source of extreme anxiety because it seemed to threaten any distinctive (non-Western) identity—which was the only proof of true equality with (rather than mere mimicry of) the West. Hence the desperate desire not just for modernity, but a distinctive modernity.

We seem to have liberated ourselves from the frustrations of this history to a large extent: now, we not only believe that there are many ways to be modern, but also claim that *our* way involves 'blending modernity with tradition' to get 'the best of both worlds'. But the seemingly self-evident clichés of today can be as misleading as the grand assertions that we have recently outgrown. Sociology suggests two rules of thumb to negotiate these terms.

First, words like 'modern' and 'traditional' must be treated as invitations, not as descriptions; they do not tell us about the character or content of the things they are attached to—they suggest the attitude we should adopt towards these things. Before we accept or decline such invitations, it is wise to look at who is issuing them and what their motives might be. Moreover, we must always remember that, even if and after we agree to label something as 'modern' or 'traditional', all the work of description and analysis still remains to be done.

Second, we must keep in mind that, given their intertwined ideological origins, the two terms almost always work in tandem, although this may not be readily visible. So, if we see one of them at work, we must search carefully for the (usually compensating) moves made by the other. For example, in order that men can be 'modern', it may be necessary for women to be 'traditional'; or if women are shown to be modern in some sphere, they may need to be shown as traditional in some other sphere. These labels may be chosen or imposed, enabling or constraining, uneventful or controversial; they may also present complex mixtures of contradictory aspects. Examining these patterns—which particular groups or spheres of society bear the costs or enjoy the benefits of such labels—provides valuable insights into the social structure.

CHAPTER THREE

The Nation as an Imagined Economy

Among the most taken-for-granted ideas of modern times, the nation has long been an enigma to social scientists because it has proved impossible to define. This may seem a rather implausible claim: surely everyone knows that a nation is a contiguous stretch of territory controlled by a single state? But such apparently robust commonsense definitions falter in the face of historical experience. If East and West Pakistan were one nation for twenty-four years without being a contiguous territory, what explains the emergence of Bangladesh as a separate nation in 1971? If contiguous territory and a single state were sufficient to make Sri Lanka or Canada a nation, why are they faced with Quebecois or Tamil nationalism? Plenty of similar counter-examples are available to subvert all the other criteria that might seem relevant, such as religion, language, race, ethnicity, and so on. There is no objective condition that is both necessary and sufficient. And even a hypothetical list of criteria that covers every existing case would still be unable to explain the birth of new nations like East Timor or the death of relatively young ones like Yugoslavia. Contrary, then, to its self-evident character in commonsense, the nation turns out to be a mysterious entity that can only be defined retrospectively and tautologically: a nation is a nation when it becomes one, and until it remains one.

This puzzling paradox received little attention in the older literature on nationalism, which tended to take the nation for granted and failed to subject the concept to rigorous scrutiny. As Sarvepalli Gopal has argued, this failure was due to a combination of ethnocentric biases and political vested interests. Although they were unaware of it at the time, the early Western thinkers on nationalism were limited by their socio-historical context. They unknowingly enabled the premature universalization of what was really a parochial, Western European notion of nationalism. Outside the West, on the other hand, nationalists engaged in anti-imperialist struggles had a vested interest in the uncritical celebration of hastily constructed notions of nation-ness that often relied on a mythical past and the out-of- context invocation of European ideas. (Gopal 1980:90-91.)

Much has changed in the decades since Gopal's survey, the most decisive change being the emergence of a new literature on nationalism characterized by its confident insistence on treating the nation as a *cultural construction*. This perspective takes nationalism to be an ideological phenomenon that does not depend on the objective reality of the commonalities it claims, such as race, ethnicity, language, religion, state, geography or history. More accurately, nationalism is seen as being capable of *inventing* these commonalities even where they do not exist, and of persuading large masses of people to have faith in these inventions. The major innovation here is that these inventions are seen not as lies that must be juxtaposed against an authentic truth, but as creative acts of a collective imagination whose workings need to be understood.

Benedict Anderson, the best known name associated with the new literature, is quite explicit about what is involved in this shift: nations must be distinguished 'not by their falsity/genuineness, but by the style in which they are imagined'. We must, therefore, rethink nationalism 'in an anthropological spirit' and treat it 'as if it belonged with "kinship" and "religion", rather than with "liberalism" or "fascism"' (Anderson 1991:15). This allows a productive shift of emphasis from the factual accuracy of the claims made on behalf of the nation to the mode in which it is imagined, what this mode permits or prevents, and the various social mechanisms that enable the crystallization and sharing of such a collectively constructed entity.

It is worth noting in passing that the shift of registers from politics and history to culture proposed by the new literature makes the study of nationalism a hospitable field for sociology and social anthropology. Indeed, the main conceptual innovation employed here—the notion of a collectively imagined institution—forms part of the founding corpus of both disciplines.[1] However, until very recently (stimulated no doubt by the recent revival of this subject in global theory), Indian sociology does not seem to have shown much interest in the nation. Among well known works, after A.R. Desai's classic dissertation study on *The social background of Indian nationalism* (first published in 1948) there is only the odd essay or two[2] before we come to the late 1990s and the work of scholars like T.K. Oommen or Dipankar Gupta. In short, although the nation is a subject that has become specially conducive to sociological and anthropological inquiry, it has not been prominent on the agenda of these disciplines in India.

But, on the other hand, it must also be pointed out that the Anderson thesis has not been very hospitable to the specificity of non-Western nationalisms. This, at any rate, is the main criticism voiced in/from India. By suggesting that the West provided the basic models which were then simply emulated in the rest of the world, theorists like Anderson discount the radically different circumstances in which nations have had to be imagined in colonial contexts. As Partha Chatterjee asked initially:

> If nationalisms in the rest of the world have to choose their imagined community from certain 'modular' forms already made available to them by Europe and the Americas, what do they have left to imagine?

Moreover, as he went on to emphasize,

> [t]he most powerful as well as the most creative results of the nationalist imagination in Asia and Africa are posited not on an identity but rather on a *difference* with the 'modular' forms

of the national society propagated by the modern West. (Chatterjee 1994:5, emphasis original.)

With hindsight, it is now clear that the initial criticism—about the Western modular forms leaving nothing to the non-Western imagination—is not as decisive as it first seemed, because the successful cultural translation and 'customization' of even a ready-made model is no mean task. But this criticism is actually a part of the subsequent argument, which is even more compelling today than when it was first made, namely, that once we recognize the specificities of non-Western (and specially ex-colonial) situations, the very notion of a 'modular' Western nationalism is thrown open to doubt. These doubts must, in turn, contend with the undeniable fact that—despite all their specificities—non-Western nations have indeed been strongly influenced by Western models, as is demonstrated, for example, by the near-universal appeal of the basic format of the nation-state or democratic governance. This has set up a field of creative tension around the question of nationalism: how different is the post-colonial non-West, and how much importance should be accorded to this difference when theorizing the nation-form?

Different Routes to Nation-ness

It is now widely accepted that Benedict Anderson's most important contribution to the study of nationalism is not his notion of an imagined community itself (this was part of received wisdom in sociology, as already mentioned), but his attention to the means—the concrete social mechanisms—with which nations are imagined into existence. This is also the most appropriate terrain, therefore, to debate the issue of the difference between Western and non-Western nationalisms.

The first and most important route to nation-ness identified by Anderson is through what he has called 'print-capitalism', or the era which saw the emergence of the printed book (and other reading materials) as mass-produced commodities. Through forms such as popular novels and daily newspapers, print-capitalism created a widely disseminable print-language that made available the technical-cultural resources for 'thinking' the nation on a historically unprecedented scale. The peculiar narrative structure of these print commodities helped to usher in the modern notion of (in Walter Benjamin's phrase) 'homogenous, empty time', where the past has no necessary relationship to the future, and both are distinct from the present. The key concept here is that of *simultaneity*—a chronological clustering that throws an otherwise unrelated set of events into common temporal containers marked and measured 'by clock and calendar' (Anderson 1983:30). This new temporal consciousness tells us that we are 'sharing the same time', and that our own experiences and those of countless unknown others are related by their contemporaneity. It is this shared knowledge of simultaneity that constitutes the first and most basic definition of a 'we', a community in the modern sense.

Thus, the citizens of a modern nation, though personally acquainted with only a microscopic minority of their compatriots, are nevertheless able to imagine the rest, to have 'complete confidence in their steady, anonymous, simultaneous activity' (Anderson 1983:31). Print capitalism, and particularly the modern novel and the daily newspaper, did a lot to cement this confidence both by the use of specific rhetorical devices that address readers as members of a (previously unrecognized) national community, and by creating shareable experiences on a mass scale. When I read the newspaper in the morning, I can be sure that hundreds of thousands of my fellow citizens will be reading the same or similar newspapers at the same time, with more or less the same 'stories'. The 'we' of nation-ness is formed precisely through such commonly known—and known to be common—experiences as reading the same news, seeing the same films, hearing the same stories … Print technology and cheap print-commodities revolutionized society by vastly expanding the number and reach of our stories-in-common, thus broadening the scope of viable communities far beyond what had been possible with the spoken word.

Although Anderson has also described other paths to nationhood,[3] print capitalism is the most emphasized, and also the most controversial. To begin with, it is interesting that Anderson's analysis of the socio-economic conditions surrounding the advent of print-as-commodity (based largely on Lucien Febvre and Henri-Jean Martin's work, *The Coming of the Book* (1976)) is restricted to the European context. On the other hand, when he moves to non-Western contexts, the commodity aspect of print-as-commodity seems to drop out, and his analysis takes the form of a reading of literary texts conducted more in the manner of a literary critic than a social scientist. The point is not that a socially sensitive literary criticism is out of place or unnecessary, but that it is surely insufficient. There can be no doubt that Anderson's suggestive readings of, say, Jose Rizal's *Noli Me Tangere* or Mas Marco Kartodikromo's *Semarang Hitam* help him to transcend narrowly European horizons, and to identify important narrative strategies for eliciting a communitarian feeling amongst readers. But these readings also need to speak to the concrete social context of the Philippines as a Spanish, or Indonesia as a Dutch, *colony*.

From a Third World perspective, Anderson's broad argument concerning print-capitalism is subject to this serious qualification. Though they may supply the technical means for visualizing the nation, when located in a colonial context, newspapers, novels and other 'print-commodities' do not translate into nationalist imaginings in any simple or automatic manner. These commodities (and all others, for that matter) are enmeshed in the specificities of the colonial context including, for example: questions of content, the size and social character of the 'reading classes', censorship, availability of printing technology, the economics of publishing, the intricate relation between colonial and native languages, and so on. As an illustration of the problems involved, consider the fact that the percentage of persons literate in any language in British India rose from 5.4 per cent in 1901 to 9.5 per cent in 1931, the corresponding figures for males only being 9.8 per cent and 15.6 per cent (Dasgupta 1987). Or consider Jawaharlal Nehru's reflections on British-Indian newspapers:

I remember that when I was a boy the British-owned newspapers in India were full of official news and utterances; of service news, transfers and promotions; of the doings of English society, of polo, races, dances, and amateur theatricals. There was hardly a word about the people of India, about their political, cultural or economic life. Reading them one would hardly suspect that they existed. (Nehru 1985:294.)

The point here is not that low levels of literacy or the skewed content of colonial newspapers makes Anderson's argument invalid, but that the *effectivity* of print-capitalism depends on whether, and in what manner, it negotiates these ground realities. Since nationalism is above all a mass phenomenon, much of the theoretical importance attached to the print medium must, in such a situation, be transferred to the social mechanisms through which nationalist feeling is *disseminated* from the literate elite to the illiterate masses.

These criticisms have been confined within the framework of Anderson's argument, but the main point is the needlessly restrictive ambit of this framework itself. Anderson is surely right to insist that nations must be distinguished by the style in which they are imagined. But he considers only a very limited set of such styles, a set that inadvertently excludes from his analysis some of the most crucial styles of the nationalist imagination in colonial countries like India. To anticipate the argument of this chapter and the one that follows, I suggest that the initial style of Indian nationalism (as that of nationalism in other colonial contexts) was a broadly anti-imperialist one. The premier idiom of this style—the most powerful theme within it—was an economic one. However, as is now becoming clear retrospectively, this initial style, despite the importance it gave to the economy, was also compatible with (or contained within itself) yet another idiom, that of Hindu communalism. Partly because of contingent events and partly because of the powerful social processes unleashed after the independence of India, the economic motif (with the developmental economy as its centrepiece) dominated over the Hindu communalist motif during the Nehru era, or roughly until the 1970s. After a protracted transition of about two decades, the contemporary era has seen the eclipse of the development motif and the resurgence of Hindu communalism in an overall context dominated by globalization.

The Economy in the Ideology of Nationalism

The market and economic relations in general have often attracted attention as contributory factors in the emergence of nations. For example, the French Marxist philosopher Henri Lefebvre has suggested that, considered spatially, the nation-form is the combined result of the geographical extent of the market and of state violence (Lefebvre 1991:112). However, this is too general and abstract a claim to be useful. For, as Etienne Balibar bluntly declares, 'It is quite impossible to "deduce" the nation form from capitalist relations of production', because these relations 'do not logically entail a single determinate form of state', and because the world market has 'an intrinsic tendency to transcend any national institutions' (Wallerstein and Balibar 1991:89). We need more concrete arguments that can offer specific reasons why market forces will tend to produce nations.

One such argument directly concerned with the non-Western experience is found in the work of Tom Nairn. His basic thesis is that the emergence of nationalism in modern world history is the consequence of the uneven development engendered by imperialistic capitalism. Resisting imperialism but nevertheless succumbing to the metropolitan fantasy of development, the colonized countries try to catch up with the West. Lacking the material and institutional resources required for development, these societies must mobilize the only resource they do have, which is the social energy that can be generated by a nationalist celebration of

> the people and the peculiarities of the region: its inherited *ethnos*, speech, folklore, skin-colour, and so on.

Third World nationalism is thus an attempt to take a 'historical short cut' to development (Nairn 1981:340).

Nairn's argument has a certain intuitive plausibility; however, when viewed from the vantage point of India, it seems that the reverse may be even more true—namely, that *development* became the 'historical short cut' to nationhood. In the Third World context, the idea of development is something much more than just a set of economic policies or processes; it is one of the crucial mechanisms that enables a national collectivity to be imagined into existence. In the most general terms, development-as-ideology helps articulate state, nation and economy, and plays a crucial role in securing the coherence of the new post-colonial nations. It provides the former colonies with a dignified and distinctive way of obeying the imperative towards a modernity that is already marked as Western. Thus, development acquired a powerful emotive-nationalist charge in India and became one of the major means for overcoming the centrifugal forces of culture, language, religion, caste or ethnicity.

There seem to be three distinct phases in which the 'imagined economy' has contributed to the making of the Indian nation. During the colonial period, the notion of an enslaved economy provides the major impetus for the nationalist struggle and gives it an all-India character. The goal of liberating the economy is seamlessly interwoven with the yearning for sovereign statehood. With independence, and specially with the advent of socialist planning, the newly liberated economy comes to be enshrined as the very essence of the emergent nation. This is the Nehruvian era of socialism, secularism and non-alignment, a period when 'the task of nation building' is taken—quite literally—to be the objective of state policy. Since the 1980s and 1990s, with the gradual weakening and finally the collapse of all three pillars of the Nehruvian utopia, we are at a juncture where the economy has a very uncertain status in the collective conception of the Indian nation.[4]

THE ENSLAVED ECONOMY: NATIONALISM, AND THE DISCOURSE OF POVERTY

One of the most striking signs marking the advent of modernity in the non-Western world is the emergence of the poverty of nations as a social scandal. Certainly the experience of poverty—its empirical presence in most parts of the globe and for large numbers—is as old as recorded history. What is new in the era of capitalist colonialism is the recognition that this is a preventable economic disorder rather than an ordained affliction. It should go without saying that this is in large part a mirror image of the discourses surrounding the wealth of Western imperial nations. As invocations of 'manifest destiny' or the 'white man's burden' begin to give way to (or at least coexist with) the realization that the Empire is 'a bread and butter question' (Cecil Rhodes) or that 'the East is a career' (Benjamin Disraeli), it is not long before Western educated ideologues in the colonies begin to assert that the wealth of the 'Mother Country' is causally related to the poverty of the 'Possessions'.

In the Indian case, the discourse of poverty is provided additional rhetorical leverage by the fact that available historical accounts (many of them from Western sources or put into circulation by the West) had been emphasizing the wealth of 'India'. In these accounts, the nation and its wealth are both equally and inseparably fabulous. For pre-modern Europe, 'India' is the legend that launched major economic pilgrimages, like those of Vasco da Gama or Christopher Columbus. With modernity, the tables are turned: the wealth of the West and the poverty of India now come to be paired in a new mythology.

With some ideological work, this reversal of fortunes could be causally related to British rule. Particularly for the early Indian nationalists, many of whom served an apprenticeship in British liberal politics, this connection, once made, could clearly be seen as violating the political ethics of the British themselves. It is this moral contradiction that led people like Dadabhai Naoroji to rail against 'un-British rule' as the cause of the 'poverty of India'. The elaboration of the arguments implied by this perspective resulted in the production of the immensely powerful theory of the economic drain. Dadabhai Naoroji's ceaseless pamphleteering and R.C. Dutt's widely influential two-volume work are emblematic products of this strain of Indian nationalism.

The less obvious but equally important aspect of the discourse of poverty is the direct help it provided in assembling the technical means for imagining the Indian nation. It has often been remarked that the British created 'India' as a meaningful administrative, political and economic entity. From the nationalist point of view, however, what is even more important is the fact that British *exploitation* helped to identify as Indian not only the national economy but also the millions of producers—peasants, artisans, and workers—who were otherwise a hopelessly disparate and fragmented constituency. By nurturing the collective recognition of a shared status as exploited producers, the nationalist movement extracted from the very apparatus of British imperialism, the concrete and practical means with which the nation could be imagined. Nationalist leaders were quite self-conscious about this aspect of British rule and its strategic uses for their cause.[5]

Commodities, Swadeshi and Patriotic Consumption

One of the concrete ways in which the economy entered the nationalist imagination, and in fact helped shape it, was through the medium of commodities. The Swadeshi movement of the last quarter of the nineteenth century and the early years of the twentieth century marks the moment when the consciousness of economic exploitation on an 'all-India' level proves catalytic for the emerging nationalist movement. As Sumit Sarkar's classic work on the politically advanced province of Bengal has shown (Sarkar 1973), the Swadeshi movement invested commodities—mundane articles of everyday use—with a new ideological charge. The middle classes were gripped by the idea that a credible claim to national identity necessarily involved explicit and visible loyalty to the national economy, even at the cost of considerable expense or inconvenience to oneself. These educated classes thus began to be active on both fronts of the Swadeshi movement, that of initiating indigenous production of hitherto imported goods, and that of boycotting the consumption or purchase of foreign goods. While by all accounts the economic impact of the Swadeshi movement appears to have been less than decisive and somewhat short lived, its ideological impact may have been significant. In the discussion that follows, I will try to indicate, very tentatively and briefly, the part played in the making of the Indian nation by commodities and the symbolic representations that they make available.

The Swadeshi movement strikingly illustrates how an invisible social process that produces its effects 'behind the backs' of social actors can be transformed into a visible one. This movement's recognition of commodities as 'social hieroglyphics' that enable the conscious invocation of the nation as (also) an economic community to which loyalty is owed, thus explicitly harnesses to the nationalist cause what is usually an unexamined part of everyday life. Right up to the days of 'traditional' capitalism, certain kinds of commodities were recognized as 'coming from' certain kinds of places. In contemporary India, although this is fast diminishing, a fairly large set of associations between particular commodities and their supposed places of origin is part of our everyday knowledge: scissors from Meerut, brass from Moradabad, silks from Benares or Kanchipuram, chappals from Kolhapur, mangoes from Ratnagiri or Banginapalli, padlocks from Aligarh ... and so on.

While late capitalism and its regime of 'flexible' accumulation have no doubt considerably weakened these traditional associations, they do seem to have played a significant part in the fashioning of a spatialized conception of the Indian nation. Commodities appear to have functioned as mnemonic devices, aids for imagining the nation in its geographical spread and specificity. Considerable work needs to be done to investigate the role played by commodities in enabling Indians to invest the idea of the nation with a concrete and specifiable geography. Here, as a preliminary illustration, are some passing remarks on the local grain mandi at Sargodha (in the Punjab) during the inter-war years taken from Prakash Tandon's autobiographical social history:

> The mandi was a big square with ground floor shops on all sides. Here the produce of the surrounding country, wheat,

cotton, millets and oilseeds came in. The farmers brought
the commodities in large carts drawn by pairs of bullocks ...
The farmers and buyers and commission agents, among them
the representatives of large European produce firms of Ralli
Brothers, Louis Drayfuss, Volkart Brothers, and their Japanese
counterparts, Toyo Menka Kaisha, Mitsu Bishi and others,
and the professional auctioneers would move from one pile
to another ... From the railway station next door, the produce
packed in gunny bags would be sent to destinations all over
the Punjab, India, and it was said, even across the seas. (Tandon
1961: 158-59.)

What is noteworthy in this account is the way in which known and
familiar local products, in their projected journeys away from the
point of production, seem to provide the means for entering and
learning to inhabit confidently what is (at least initially) an unknown
and unfamiliar mental geography—'the Punjab', 'India', and even
the world beyond. That representatives from European and Japanese
produce firms were present in the Sargodha mandi would surely have
assisted in the formation of initial notions of national boundaries.
Such contacts through the world of commodities are particularly
notable because, for the average Indian resident of even a medium-
sized town leave alone the villages, actual encounters with the British
(or other Europeans) were rare. As Tandon points out, this time about
his ancestral hometown of Gujrat in northwest Punjab (now in
Pakistan), Englishmen were seldom seen by Indians:

After sixty years, we in Gujrat had almost forgotten that we
were ruled by the British. In the city you never saw an
Englishman except some rare salesman throwing free
cigarettes out of a tonga to promote the habit of smoking. You
had to go out of the city gates into the Civil Station to see one
of the three or four Englishmen posted in Gujrat, the Deputy
Commissioner, the Superintendent of Police, sometimes the
Executive Engineer, possibly the Sessions Judge, and perhaps
the Padre Sahib. (Tandon 1961:122-23.)

Thus, contact through the medium of commodities appears to have been much more important for the majority of the population who did not actually meet foreigners except on ceremonial or other unusual occasions. While the image of an Englishman 'throwing free cigarettes out of a tonga' is a particularly striking one, more typical instances of encounters with the 'outside world' were probably those involving commodities in the marketplace. Of course, commodities functioned as two-way linkages: Indians encountered the larger world (both intra- as well as inter-national) through commodities not only as sellers but also as buyers. Here is Tandon once again on his first experience of the attractions of foreign-made goods found in the market on the main street of Gujrat:

> The goods were usually British or German, and many of the brands had become household names. Japan had not quite entered the market. One could buy knives, scissors, buttons, cotton and silk thread, mirrors, soaps, bottled hair oils, razors, socks, woollen and cotton knitwear, etc. These imported things always held more glamour for us than the local ones. We preferred the imported combs to the hand-made wooden ones, the electroplated Sheffield and Solingen knives and scissors to the solid steel ones made by our local smiths, Pears and Vinolia soap to the home-boiled desi soap, and the shining coloured buttons to the simple cloth ones. (Tandon 1961:110-11.)

The glamour of 'imported' things, not quite a thing of the past even in contemporary India, took on an added dimension when the product in question visibly incorporated the legendary technology of the West. Tandon recalls the first encounter with one such commodity, also famous for having won the admiration of as staunch a critic of modern technology as Mahatma Gandhi:

> Perhaps in celebration of father's recovery [from a near-fatal attack of influenza during an epidemic], or because the time was ripe for it otherwise, the first mechanical contraption arrived in our house. It was the Singer sewing machine,

shining black and chromium-plated, with a highly polished case in wood. Few homes as yet possessed one. With it came a colourful calendar showing Singer's popularity in different countries of the world. This was my first introduction to people of other races, if only in pictures. (Tandon 1961:162.)

It was the glamour of the imported commodity and the mystique of Western technology that the Swadeshi movement had to confront in its attempt to bring a national consciousness into the marketplace. Of course, the two commodities with which the movement had its greatest political successes, namely salt and cloth, were neither particularly glamourous nor associated with a technology that seemed decisively beyond reach. They were no doubt chosen for political reasons—because they touched the life of every Indian, and because their production was very well distributed across the length and breadth of the country, specially in the case of indigenous textiles. But the ideological paradigm out of which Swadeshi emerged included as its core element the imperative to catch up with Western technology and science so that this superior material culture could be assimilated and married to the already superior spiritual side of Indian culture, thereby laying the foundation for the re-emergence of India as a great nation on the world stage.

Partha Chatterjee associates this basic ideological paradigm with the work of Bankimchandra Chattopadhyay, and terms it the 'moment of departure' of Indian nationalist discourse. Writing in 1888, Bankim proposes the concept of *Anusilan*, or 'a "system of culture", more complete and more perfect than the western concept of culture', to be fashioned by borrowing from the West those knowledges (of the world and of the self) in which they were superior, and joining these to the kind of knowledge (that of God) in which the East was undoubtedly superior. This was the philosophical basis for Bankim's declaration that:

The day European industries and sciences are united with Indian *dharma* … the Hindus will gain a new life and become

powerful like the English under Cromwell or the Arabs under
Muhammad. (Quoted in Chatterjee 1986: 66.)

The point to note about the Swadeshi movement is the way in which
commodities acquired the potential of becoming crucial mnemonic
devices, serving to invoke in convenient shorthand an entire
nationalist philosophy. The movement touched such products as brass
utensils, nibs for pens, cutlery, china, soap, perfumes, shoes, boots and
leather products, matches, buttons, cigarettes, ink, paper, candles, sugar
and edible oils, not counting the staple of textiles both silk and cotton.
This, too, is to concentrate on the identifiable products and to ignore
significant (though often short-lived) efforts in banking, insurance,
shipping and technical education. Thus, though Sarkar tells us that 'A
sense of anti-climax is difficult to avoid in any survey of swadeshi
business achievements' (1973: 134), in the context of the argument of
this chapter, it should be clear that commodities played a central role
in this movement, which, in turn, was crucial in the development of
nationalist consciousness.

The Swadeshi movement, by anticipating much of Gandhian
economics, made it possible to think of the nation as also *a locus of
production*, and to look at commodity relations as also implying certain
mutual social and moral responsibilities. Indeed, it was precisely the
imperial regime's refusal of these responsibilities—the classic case is
that of the ruin of Indian handlooms by the textile industry of
Lancashire—that had precipitated the self-consciousness of subject
status. In the nationalist imagination, swaraj, no matter how or when
it came, necessarily had to be different from the imperial regime. Hence
the appeal of the Gandhian model, with its emphasis on social relations
and mutual responsibility in defiance of the impersonal laws of the
market. Hence also the ideological paradigm of Nehruvian socialism
which enshrines the economy as the embodiment of the nation, and
installs the figure of the producer-patriot as its chief deity.

THE ECONOMY ENSHRINED: DEVELOPMENT PLANNING IN THE NEHRU ERA

Much has already been written about the relative merits and the points of comparison and contrast between the Gandhian and the Nehruvian models of national development. It may also be useful to think of them as prescriptions for the imagination, as alternative ways of visualizing the nation and its future.

As against Bankim's utopia integrating *both* traditional culture and modern economy, the Gandhian and Nehruvian alternatives emphasize only one. Nehru's option is the one that is more in keeping with the tenor of the times, in which a modern economy is paired with a modernized culture that has left behind most of its conservative traditional beliefs and attitudes. Gandhi's vision is the more radical and novel one: he wishes not only to revitalize traditional culture but also to have it govern the economy—he is happy to sacrifice the alleged benefits of a modernity driven by science and technology. Thus, the Nehruvian and Gandhian models are hybrid variants of the original nationalist paradigm based on the separation of culture and economy.[6] Being hybrids, both models share the same general relationship to the fundamental economy-culture axis of Indian nationalism. This is a relationship marked, on the one hand, by the ability to develop and maximize the ideological effect of one of the poles of the basic axis, and, on the other hand, an unavoidable vulnerability with respect to the other pole of the axis.

Thus, the Nehruvian model is able to optimize the ideological impact of the idea of a modern industrialized economy by developing it into a powerful vision of the future of the Indian nation. However, despite its best efforts, this vision is not able to allay doubts regarding the cultural content of the kind of national identity it offers. In an analogous manner, the Gandhian alternative succeeds brilliantly in giving voice to the ideas of the Indian nation in an idiom that strikes deep cultural chords: Gandhi is credited with almost single-handedly 'inviting the masses into history'. But the economic programme espoused by this model proves to be too radical for the times, and is unable to shake off the label of an irrational and anachronistic attitude to modern technology and the charge of wanting to distribute poverty rather than aiming for mass prosperity.

It is important to remember that the Nehruvian model did not have to invent wholesale the ideological construct of an industrialized nation; rather, it gave shape to an already existing consensus that informed the early nationalist movement. This widespread sentiment about the need for developing modern industries in India was a strong and deeply felt one; it was not dissuaded by the awareness of the evils of Western industrialism, or by sympathy for the village crafts of the country. Indeed, Justice Ranade, one of the most ouspoken and influential advocates of industrialization, went so far as to declare that only modern industry could unite the diverse peoples of India into a cohesive nation.[7]

Gandhi's attempt to infuse the idea of a non-modern economy with a positive moral charge represents a new and revolutionary interpretation of the nationalist paradigm. This is the unexpected intervention, one that has the potential of breaking out of the ideological constraints of the times. The notion of a just and humane economy, where commodity relations are minimized if not eliminated altogether, directly confronts Bankim's desire for a strong and powerful economy along Western lines. However, it should be emphasized that Gandhi's objection to modern industry and technology is even more radical than it appears because it is based on an objection to exchange relations themselves, which to him are the root of all evil beginning with exploitation. Ideally, he would like to abolish exchange value altogether, and live by the principles of use value—i.e., fulfilling one's personal needs through one's own labour (Chatterjee 1986:85-93).[8]

How, then, did the Nehruvian model of the economy 'win' this ideological contest for shaping the idea of the Indian nation, even if it was a one-sided contest? The answer must be sought in factors like development economics and socialist planning.

Development Planning as Ideological Device

Between them, socialist planning and its liberal-Western analogue, development economics, offered a remarkable array of resources for representing the basic economic issues facing the countries of Asia and Africa which gained independence in the mid-twentieth century. Interestingly, both paradigms were particularly amenable to translation into a specifically *nationalist* idiom; moreover, and this probably accounts for the predominantly economic rhetoric of Third World nationalism in mid-century, they were both unambiguous in identifying the *economy* as the single most important (and often the only) arena for social action. These discursive formations were specially helpful for the populist side (since they promised the end of exploitation and poverty, an egalitarian society, etc.), and the modernist side (because of their invocation of modern science and technology, including the apparatus of scientific economic planning) of nationalist rhetoric. Needless to say both played up to the 'catching-up-with-the-West' syndrome afflicting all non-Western and specially Third World nations.

The circumstances under which the Nehruvian model was installed in India beginning with the Second Five Year Plan following the adoption of the famous 'socialistic pattern of society' resolution at the Avadi session of the All India Congress Committee in 1955 are well known. What is important here is the question of the specific modes in which this model made it possible—indeed, even necessary—to imagine the nation.

If commodities can be used, sometimes unconsciously, as mnemonic aids in imagining the nation, the apparatus of economic planning is explicitly predicated upon a mental construct of the national economy. This construction of the economy very soon becomes synonymous with the nation itself. This enshrining of the economy as that part of the nation which stands for the whole was perhaps one of Nehru's distinctive personal contributions to the nationalist cause. The Indian variant of development planning initiated by the Feldman-Mahalanobis model for the Second Plan was particularly suitable for such discursive purposes because of its emphasis on 'physical planning'. This made it very easy to anthropomorphize the economy and to treat it as a sort of person writ large, in much the same way as Hindu gods and goddesses are thought of: as superhuman personalities, nevertheless endowed with distinctly human traits and peculiarities of character.

The explicit mapping of national resources and coordination of projected targets that a plan requires is clearly much more 'efficient' than occasional encounters with commodities in evoking the extra-sensory entity that the nation represents. Moreover, harking back to Anderson, the centrality of the temporal element in all development planning also provides a direct and powerful means of evoking a 'homogeneous time', a time which is not 'empty' but is punctuated by a coherent national narrative. A 'five-year-plan' is thus a newspaper multiplied many times over in terms of its impact on the individual's ability to imagine a collective project that is the nation. In short, planning may perhaps be thought of as helping to produce a scientific-technical analogue to the figure of 'Bharat Mata'.

How is such a figure to be imagined—in what form will 'she' become visible to us? Once again Nehru seems to provide the answer: the nation becomes visible to us in all the various tasks of nation building that are being undertaken by the Indian people and state during this phase. For obvious reasons, giant steel plants or gigantic dams and power stations are the most privileged sites where the nation emerges into our consciousness. Here is Nehru on the Bhakra Nangal dam:

> Our engineers tell us that probably nowhere else in the world is there a dam as high as this. The work bristles with difficulties and complications. As I walked around the site I thought that these days the biggest temple and mosque and gurdwara is the place where man works for the good of mankind. Which place can be greater than this, this Bhakra Nangal, where thousands and lakhs of men have worked, have shed their blood and sweat and laid down their lives as well? Where can

be a greater and holier place than this, which we can regard as higher? …

I look far, not only towards Bhakra Nangal, but towards this our country, India, whose children we are. Where is she going? Where have we to lead her, which way have we to walk and what mighty tasks have we to undertake? Some of these will be completed in our lifetime. Others will be taken up and completed by those who come after us. The work of a nation or a country is never completed. It goes on and no one can arrest its progress—the progress of a living nation. (Nehru 1980: 214)

There are two things which are striking about the above passage. One is the conspicuous interweaving of religion and the economy—the dam is explicitly claimed to be a holy place, and the task of nation building a religious responsibility. This move captures the characteristic feature of the Nehruvian model, namely its attempt to bring together the commitment to building a modern and industrialized nation with the impulse towards modernizing—dare one say secularizing?—the national culture. The invocation of religious feeling at such a 'non-traditional' site as a hydroelectric project serves to shift the terrain on which this feeling has hitherto been situated, while simultaneously signalling that national construction projects are to be invested with the faith, piety and fervour previously reserved for religious works.

The second noteworthy feature is the strong link that is constantly being established between patriotism and work. The theme of work is continually emphasized (specially its difficulties, its scale, its limitlessness …) even as the object of this work is asserted to be the nation itself. The nation is not only the locus for all this work, but it is also the end towards which this work is moving: patriotism is quite literally the act of building a nation. This is another typical feature of the Nehruvian model, the nexus between patriotism and production. In fact, it may be argued that the protagonist of this model of national development is the producer-patriot. However, this particular aspect of the Nehruvian model can perhaps be better appreciated when contrasted with features of the contemporary situation.

The Significance of the Nehruvian Era

The Nehruvian era amply demonstrates the centrality of the economy for the nationalism of the time. The major spatial strategy of this era is to foreground the economy—the nation is figured primarily as an economic space. It is this economic geography that the post-independence generation has grown up with. Powerfully disseminated through schools and all the state media, the nation becomes a space of production, and is imagined via economic associations. Places are named, so to speak, economically: Kodarma is 'mica', Ankleshwar is 'petroleum', Rourkela is 'steel', Bhakra Nangal is 'power', Coimbatore is 'textiles' and so on. These 'sites of development' were the principal heterotopias fashioned by the Nehruvian regime. They invited the citizens of the new nation to see themselves reflected in the mirror of technological progress and development, and to identify themselves as fellow travellers on the journey towards this common goal. The telos of development is thus not unlike that of the pilgrimage, and indeed, the comparison is often explicitly invoked.

When compared to the sacred geography of Hindutva (to be discussed in the next chapter), this spatial vision appears to be remarkably inclusive, even if ideologically naïve in its substitution of socio-economic for religious-cultural identities. But closer scrutiny proves that exclusions are being practised here as well, except that they operate along very different axes. Though it is yet to be written, a new spatial history of Nehruvian developmentalism—which goes beyond the naïvëty of treating 'regional imbalances' as merely another failure of plan implementation—will no doubt uncover the multidimensional relations of domination established along the inter-regional, rural-urban, and city-megacity axes. In the most obvious case, this spatial logic is surely at least partly responsible for a variety of contemporary regional-ethnic movements, from those in the North-East to Punjab, Kashmir, Jharkhand, and Uttaranchal. However, the precise ways in which this causality works may not be obvious, as the instructive contrast between Punjab and Jharkhand indicates. If the former demonstrates the discontents that successful development can produce, the latter, as the locus *par excellence* of the Nehru-Mahalanobis model of development based on heavy industries, illustrates the axiom that 'development' need not erase the backwardness of the region where it occurs. Jharkhand contains five major steel plants or virtually all of India's steel industry; most of the major coal, iron ore and mica mines; and several large heavy engineering and chemical plants. Also located here is the nation's largest integrated river valley project for hydroelectric power generation and irrigation. (All this does not even begin to account for the varied forest-based products of the region.) Yet, Jharkhand and its original inhabitants remain backward and extremely poor.

While hindsight may have exposed it as (at worst) a fraud or (at best) an illusion, we still need to ask how Nehruvian developmentalism managed to seem so inclusive to so many for so long. Despite their apparently self-evident status, it may still be useful to focus attention on 'development' and 'nation' as the two main planks on which the hegemonic consensus of this era was erected. More precisely, Nehruvian hegemony was the product of the synergistic union of these ideas—their ideological 'cementing'—by the nationalist movement in India during the first half of the twentieth century. The interweaving of 'development' and 'nation' produced a strong and durable ideological fabric, one side of which might be called 'the developing nation' and the other 'national development'. This pair worked to deflect the scepticism generated by either concept towards the other: questions of national identity were referred to 'development', and doubts about the development process were referred to 'the nation'.

Given that in India the nation was visualized specifically as a community of patriotic producers, the Nehruvian nation-space could identify as the 'other' only the shirker—i.e., the person who refused to participate in the collective task of 'nation building'. It is in this sense that the Nehruvian nation-space seems to be inclusive, because the 'other' has no particular *cultural* identity, except the generic one of the anti- or non-modernist. By contrast, Hindutva claimed a nation-space where the major axis of exclusion is cultural—the 'others' who arouse anxiety are indelibly marked by an essential cultural difference.

However, the other side of the apparent inclusiveness of the Nehruvian nation-space was an elitism that operated in a universalistic (rather than particularistic) mode. If the 'other' was culturally unmarked, so was the dominant group.[9] Thus, the Nehruvian era created and privileged a pan-Indian elite that could, by and large, afford to cut loose its regional moorings. Not only did this elite seem to be 'placeless', it also appeared to be 'caste-less' and 'class-less': a truly secular, modern elite. It spoke in the modernist idiom of secular nationalism, scientific technology, and economic development; by adopting this idiom, the elite was able to render invisible its own ascriptive markers. The fact that it was almost exclusively upper caste and middle class, and that it came from a very select cultural background and a specific set of regions could become 'transparent' and thus be made to vanish. Consisting of the rising technocracy, the professional-managerial class, intellectuals and top bureaucrats, this was an elite which thought of itself in purely 'national' terms, whose native habitat was the de-territorialised space called New Delhi, where it sometimes seemed as though 'only those people who are unable to speak any Indian language are the real repositories of Indian nationalism' (Kaviraj 1990:69).

The Chinese war marked the beginning of the end of the Nehruvian era; it not only discredited Nehru as a statesman, but also re-legitimized the jingoistic, partition-era rhetoric of the Hindu right. The long simmering discontent among the marginalized power brokers and regional elites surfaced with Nehru's death, which also coincided with a break in the process of planned development brought about by war, drought and an economic crisis. Indira Gandhi could take control of the Congress only by splitting it, and her reign inevitably marked the advent of the era of electoral arithmetic based on vote banks and an implicit communal logic.

The inclusive spatial sense of Nehruvian developmentalism was overtaken by an anxiety about the vulnerability of the borders of the nation. At the same time, the ideological privileges bestowed on 'national' developmental projects could no longer be maintained. They had to negotiate with the more immediate and localized sense of social space in the form of several 'sons of the soil' movements (specially around public-sector jobs), as well as movements projecting assertive regional identities that refused any longer to dissolve easily into the national. As the hegemony of Nehruvianism crumbled, the nation-space became increasingly vulnerable to contestations, specially since neither the official notion of secularism nor the Nehruvian vision of the national community had strong local roots. With the dream of egalitarian economic development becoming more and more implausible, new ways of visualizing the nation-space began to compete for control of the ideological high ground within civil society.

AFTER DEVELOPMENT: THE CONTEMPORARY ERA

The decline of Nehruvian developmentalism seems to suggest that the economy can no longer function as an important ideological resource for imagining the nation. Two main developments underline this assessment: the resurgence of Hindutva as an alternative mode of imagining the Indian nation; and the 'pro-globalization' economic policies that have been followed with remarkable uniformity by very different political regimes since the 1990s.

Since their remarkable revival in the last two decades, the Sangha Parivar organizations have made a sustained effort to shift the terrain for the definition of patriotism from the economy to religious-communal identity. In the Nehruvian model, the identity of a patriot was (at least in principle if not always in practice) available to anyone able and willing to participate in the task of nation building. Today, the Hindu right wing organizations are suggesting that patriotism ought to be a matter of blood rather than actions, and that the attributes one acquires by birth (such as membership of a particular religious community) should take precedence over everything else. It is this logic that assumes that a Hindu 'NRI'—who may contribute nothing to the country or its economy—is nevertheless a patriot, while a Muslim who may have lived and worked in India all his life is by definition a potential traitor.

The new economic policies, too, have weakened the earlier paradigm in their own way. In the current policy regime, only those producers are valued who produce for the global market and bring in foreign exchange. Thus, it is not a producer's ability to satisfy the needs of the nation, but rather his/her ability to respond to the needs of an abstract 'global market' that is decisive. At a different level, the patriotic producer is no longer the most celebrated category, this position having been taken over by the 'cosmopolitan consumer'. As the advertising world reminds us insistently, the imagination of the new India is dominated by visions of participating in global consumption patterns. We are invited to take patriotic pride in the fact that, at long last, prosperous 'upper middle-class' Indians are able to consume exactly the same 'world class' products and brands that are available to privileged Western consumers.

This is not to suggest, however, that Hindutva and globalization were solely responsible for the decline of Nehruvian developmentalism—as discussed above, the internal problems of this paradigm were also significant. It is precisely these kinds of interactional effects that are very difficult to sort out when studying contemporary events without the luxury of historical distance. Subsequent chapters will discuss the impact of Hindutva and of globalization, but the fact remains that the contemporary era is a volatile and uncertain one, particularly where matters of identity are concerned. Even if we no longer entertain naïve expectations about the disappearance of the nation-state or of nationalism in the era of globalization, the times are certainly pushing us to consider the possibility of 'post-patriotic' identities driven by supra-national ideas and institutions. How one imagines the nation, it would seem, is no longer as important as how one imagines the globe and one's place in it.

CHAPTER FOUR

Hindutva and its Spatial Strategies

It could be by sheer coincidence that new ways of thinking about the social aspects of space have emerged at around the same time as new ways of theorizing the nation as discussed in the last chapter ('The Nation as an Imagined Economy'). But the significant overlap between the two literatures suggests otherwise. Contemporary social theory has begun to reconsider both space and nation in ways which attempt to go beyond (or at least to sidestep) the traditional dichotomy between the material and the mental, the objective and the subjective. Thus, if the post-Anderson literature on the nation-form has concentrated on how nations are collectively imagined, the 'reassertion of space in critical social theory' has led us to the realization that even such a physical phenomenon as space is not 'natural' but is *socially produced*.[1]

There is an obvious meeting ground for both strands of theory in the fact that an identifiable *territory* is a necessary (though not a sufficient) condition for the birth of a nation. But this territory or space is simultaneously abstract (imagined, mental) and concrete (physical, geographical). These contrary aspects of the nation-as-space are linked because they both exist in the social imagination, and ultimately, in the minds of people. However, this link is not pre-given, it must be painstakingly constructed. Nations take shape—they become socially visible—only when an abstract ideological terrain and a concrete physical territory can be cross-mapped on to each other to produce a sense of nation-ness that large numbers of people share and believe in. Even after it has been successfully produced, this sense of nation-ness needs to be continually nurtured, partly through efforts to ensure that ideology and geography stay in synch with each other.[2] Such attempts to connect subjective/mental and objective/physical notions of space are being called *spatial strategies* in this chapter.

Long before it adopted the garb of a modern nation, 'India' first appeared on the Western world map as the fabled space of imperial desire—the legendary land that inspired the economic piligrimages of explorers like Christopher Columbus or Vasco da Gama. Imperialism, after all, is the spatial ideology *par excellence*. Predicated on the ability to fuse abstract spaces and concrete places into a political agenda, it is born (in the words of Edward Said) '[a]t the moment when a coincidence occurs between real control and power, the *idea* of what a given place was (could be, might become), and an *actual* place' (Said 1993:78, emphasis added).

But the colony is also the site of a struggle, no matter how unequal, between colonizer and colonized. For the same coincidence of idea, place and power provides ideological resources 'both for Westerners taking possession of land and, during decolonization, for resisting natives reclaiming it'. (Said 1993:78.) Thus, imperialism and colonialism establish a spatial order and a territorial ideology that are then selectively utilized by an emergent nationalism to fashion its own spatial strategies.

The social history of the map provides an interesting illustration of the dual role of nationalism as both the antagonist and the inheritor of imperialism. Nationalism claims the imperial map as its legitimate legacy, but radically transforms the moral meaning of this map (Smith 1986:202). The first step in this transformation is almost invariably the invention of antiquity, the retroactive projection of a modern nation into an ancient past as timeless as it is perfect (Smith 1986:183). In this way, time is used to change the meaning of space—the nationalist map, itself borrowed from imperialism, is invested with a hoary, pre-Western history. With this moral repositioning, the colonial map can be simultaneously appropriated and abrogated, while colonial rule is treated as a recent and momentary aberration in the 'great and ancient tradition' of the colonized nation.

In the construction of the nation as a special kind of imagined space, the historical (or more accurately 'historicized') map is followed by what Benedict Anderson has called the 'second avatar' of the map, the map-as-logo. Among the significant methods which enabled the linking of a particular physical geography to a specific imagined community as its homeland, the logo-map was given a major boost by new print technology which enabled its cheap mass production, allowing it to function as a 'pure sign' (or symbol) rather than as a 'compass to the world'.[3]

More generally, nationalist spatial strategies attempted to translate the 'facts' of geography into matters of patriotic faith and, ultimately, received experience. The most obvious manifestation of this in the Indian case is the figure of 'Mother India'. Our national anthem provides another example of a straightforward spatial strategy for meshing a particular geography—the physical features of the Indian subcontinent—with a specific ideology, Indian nationalism. '... *Punjab, Sindhu, Gujarata, Maratha / Dravida, Utkala, Vanga / Vindhya, Himachala, Jamuna, Ganga ...*' Only a tiny minority of Indians will have direct personal experience of all these regions, rivers and mountain ranges; but Rabindranath's anthem invites us all to feel a patriotic sense of proprietorship and pride in all of them, even those we may never ever see in our lifetime.

Spatial strategies tie an imagined space to a real place in such a way that these ties also bind the people addressed by the strategy to particular identities, and the political/practical consequences that they entail. But the important point about them is that they have to operate in a resistant medium—they must engage in ideological battle with rival (or prior) strategies that may have already established a different set of links between spaces and places. Thus, nationalist spatial strategies had to contend not only with imperialist and colonialist ones but also had to overcome the resistance offered by other ways of thinking about community, like regional parochialism, religious chauvinism and so on.

Moreover—and this point is crucial for the present discussion—nationalist spatial strategies were themselves hardly homogenous, since Indian nationalism was not a single monolithic entity. Two kinds of nationalism were particularly important in India, one based on religious-communal identities and the other on a more explicitly economic ideology of development (as discussed in the previous chapter). These strands have not been mutually exclusive—indeed, at the level of political rhetoric, there was almost always a significant overlap since each claimed (albeit with more or less stridency at different times) that it incorporated the other. Nevertheless, they represent distinct dialects within nationalist discourse deploying different spatial ideologies.

This chapter is an attempt to understand the spatial strategies of *hindutva*, the term being used here as an abbreviation for both the general ideology associated with, and the socio-political movement led by, the neo-Hindu right-wing groups who belong to what they call the 'Sangh Parivar', the coalition of organizations led by the Rashtriya Swayamsevak Sangh (RSS).[4] The spatial strategies of hindutva have had a significant impact on contemporary Indian society and politics. They have sought to redefine the nation-space by rearticulating the link between the imagined community and its territorial domain. Such rearticulations, I shall argue, have attempted to prise loose the nation-space from its moorings in alternative ideologies in order to relocate it within the framework of Hindu hegemony.

Historical Hindutva: Savarkar and the Nation as Holy Land

There was nothing inherent in nationalist spatial strategies that prevented their use by groups based on religious or regional identities.

Indeed, there were areas in which religious groups—specially Hindus—were at a significant advantage, because they could build on the powerful base of sacred geographies. Given the absence of any *national* community that was supra- or non-religious, attempts to construct an 'imagined community' had to fall back on whatever existed in living memory that could be used to help concretize this new and unfamiliar notion. Thus, even self-consciously non-communal nationalists could not afford to ignore the mnemonic aids and powerful, long-familiar metaphors offered by the popular sense of history and geography, a sense inevitably inflected by religion.[5]

Moreover, the concept as well as the concrete political identity of 'nationalism' was flexible enough to permit communalists to not only claim but also to sincerely believe that theirs was a truly nationalist rather than a sectarian group. Matters were further complicated by the late nineteenth century religious revivalism, specially within Hinduism, which attempted with partial success to yoke together modernist ideals (science, rationality, technology, progress) and a reformed religious-spiritual creed that downplayed the more atavistic and contradictory aspects of religion (untouchability, the subordination of women, superstition or excessive ritualism). With the advent of this new 'improved' variety of religious identity, it did not seem so self-evident as it had before that one had to *choose* between religion and spirituality on the one hand, and the ideals of modernity and science on the other.[6] It is in this context that we have to examine the impact of Savarkar's distinctly modern Hindu communalism[7] on spatial ways of thinking about the Indian nation.

SAVARKAR'S *HINDUTVA*[8]

'Hindutva is not a word but a history' declares Savarkar at the beginning of his political pamphlet, even as he proceeds to show how this history is closely and crucially intertwined with a *geography* (p.2ff). He is very clear that the term which he did more than anyone else to popularize, and which is enjoying a major revival today—hindutva, or 'Hindu-ness'—is not to be confused with Hindu*ism*, the latter being a 'sectarian' term, referring to the followers of the Hindu religion proper. Hindutva, on the other hand, includes members of other 'Indic' faiths like Sikhism, Buddhism, or Jainism, though it insists on excluding all other faiths regardless of their presence in India for several centuries.

Savarkar invokes the etymology of the word 'Hindu'—derived from the Sanskrit 'Sindhu', the name of the river otherwise known as the Indus, and also the word for ocean. He recounts a story in which Aryan tribes from Central Asia came to settle in the Indus basin, and subsequently spread out into the entire subcontinent while managing to retain their sense of nation-ness and cultural identity, until 'the valorous Prince of Ayodhya made triumphant entry in Ceylon and actually brought the whole land from the Himalayas to the seas under one sovereign sway' (pp. 7-8).

This established the true geographical boundaries of the 'Sindhu' nation, from 'Atak to Cuttack', and from the 'Himalayas to the Cape'— or, more classically, from 'Sindhu to Sindhu', or 'river (Indus) to (the two) oceans'. Savarkar takes great pains to stress these boundaries, and specially the versatility of the sanctified word *Sindhu*.[9] The reason for the excessive concern for these boundaries soon becomes obvious when his criteria for determining hindutva are announced. These are stated as the three conditions of *pitrabhoo*, *jati*, and *sanskriti*. The first insists that a 'Hindu' should be born within Hindustan and thus have a legitimate claim to this nation-space as the fatherland. The second makes it obligatory for a Hindu to inherit Hindu 'blood' through natural parents.[10] But the most crucial interpretive move is in the third criterion, namely that of a shared culture or *sanskriti*. Savarkar very quickly shifts from the common meanings of culture to a very specific one, namely, allegiance to a particular sacred geography. Thus, the final and ultimately all-important criterion for being a Hindu is that one's *punyabhoo* or holy land should coincide with the *pitrabhoo* so carefully demarcated earlier.

Savarkar's essentially territorial test for defining a 'Hindu' is thus based on the claim to a sacred geography. Among the three criteria that he proposes, it is clear that *punyabhoo* takes precedence over *pitrabhoo* and *jati*. In fact, it is easily demonstrated that the latter two criteria are neither necessary nor sufficient: the case of a hypothetical American who may become a Hindu (p.54) demonstrates that blood and fatherland are not essential; while the fate of the Christians and Muslims of India (p.72), who are excluded despite their fulfilment of both these criteria, shows that they are certainly not sufficient. These instances establish beyond doubt that the criterion of *punyabhoo* is both necessary and sufficient, making it the only relevant condition. This conclusion is further reinforced by the highly significant *exceptions* that Savarkar considers—the Sindhis, and emigrant Indians settled abroad. The Sindhis are conferred membership on the basis of textual interpretation to the effect that *both* banks of the Indus are to be included within the borders of Hindustan. As for emigrants, they are to be considered Hindus no matter where they are because of their holy lands being in Hindustan.[11]

Savarkar's thesis asserts that only those marked by hindutva have the moral-political right to constitute the nation, since their secular and religious-cultural interests are presumed to refer to the same geographical space. The basic spatial strategy behind Savarkar's notion of hindutva is the redefinition of the nation as a sacred space: the claim that the nation is, and ought to be, formed in the shape of a *punyabhoo*, a holy land. This serves to invest the Indian nation with a religious essence—an un-analysable, un-questionable sacred value—that 'outsiders' can never experience or comprehend, and which forever and completely defines 'insiders'.

It is important to note that the basic premises of the *punyabhoo* model continue to be relevant today in a variety of contexts that go far beyond the narrowly communal. Thus, David Mandelbaum has argued that the Hindu epics and legends which 'teach that the stage for the gods was nothing less than the entire land' provide an important traditional basis for a sense of national identification, a sense continually confirmed through pilgrimage. (Mandelbaum 1972:401, quoted in Van der Veer 1996:120.) Emphasizing the importance of pilgrimages in particular, Peter Van der Veer suggests that their significance may have increased in the colonial and post-colonial periods. Greater prosperity among the landowning classes and the emergence of a secure urban elite went along with unprecedented improvements in the communication and transport infrastructure to increase the frequency and scope of pilgrimages. Moreover, 'Western discourse on the nation as a territorially based community colluded with religious discourse on sacred space' to influence the geographical dimension of the nation idea (Van der Veer 1996:122).

A telling anecdote illustrates the potency of this strategy: in the 1959 border negotiations with China, Jawaharlal Nehru argued that India's borders were not colonial creations, but had been part of her 'culture and tradition for the past two thousand years or so', while a White Paper on this subject (prepared by the Foreign Ministry) invoked support from the *Rig Veda*, the Mahabharata, and the Ramayana.[12]

THE NEHRUVIAN INTERRUPTION

As recognized by many scholars, the mainstream of the Indian national movement led by the Congress included a broad spectrum of tendencies that based themselves on implicit or explicit appeals to Hindu religion.[13] These ranged from the militantly communal stance of a Tilak or a Savarkar to the much more complex but nevertheless recognizably Hindu approach of Gandhi. Indeed, as Nehru notes in his autobiography, the explicitly secular tendency within the Congress (as different from tendencies that believed in coalitional arrangements across communities, specially Hindu-Muslim unity) was a relatively weak one, its main proponent being Nehru himself. Given these conditions, it is difficult to say what the specific course of our post-independence history would have been were it not for two critical events.

The assassination of Mahatma Gandhi by Nathuram Godse, and the latter's links with the RSS stigmatized the Hindu right and relegated it to the sidelines of national politics for more than a decade. Similarly, the sudden death of Sardar Vallabhbhai Patel in 1950 left the communal right within the Congress leaderless, and paved the way for the emergence of Nehru as the undisputed leader of the party, enabling him to play a decisive role in post-independence India.

The period from independence up to the mid-1960s—the Nehruvian era—has to be understood in the light of these events. If this era is now seen as the golden age of secularism, it is mainly due to the successful 'regionalizing' of communalism during this period, specially in the northern heartland and the west. The 'golden age' of secularism was predicated not so much on the defeat of communalism but its *repression* and *displacement* from the national public sphere.

If the nation-space in Savarkar's hindutva was based on a sacred geography, the Nehruvian nation-space was shaped by an *economic geography*. This was in keeping with Nehru's essentially economistic understanding of communalism. Nehru believed that the legal guarantee of equality of citizenship regardless of religion, caste, creed or other social attributes would render communalism obsolete. By refusing to guarantee this equality, the colonial state was keeping communalism alive in order to play off one community against another. A national state would remedy this, and thus end religious conflicts: 'Class conflicts there might well be, but not religious conflicts, except in so far as religion itself represented some vested interest'.[14] It was this Nehruvian confidence about the irrelevance of religion as a social problem of the future that was shattered in the 1980s with the resurgence of Hindu communalism.

Contemporary Hindutva and its Spatial Strategies

A first approximation of the overall spatial character of hindutva is that it is an attempt to reverse the spatial logic of Nehruvianism in order to return to Savarkar's vision of the nation-space. If Nehru claimed that dams and steel plants were the temples of modern India, hindutva stands him on his head and insists that temples are to contemporary India what steel plants and dams were to Nehruvian India.

The socio-spatial dimensions of communalism as a process of 'competitive de-secularization' (Vanaik 1993), involve an effort to re-sacralize the nation-space. De-secularization is directly dependent upon the strategic deployment of essentialism. It is in the name of religious essences—un-analysable, un-contestable claims that are treated as self-evident truths by the faithful—that state secularism is denounced for its attempt to treat all faiths alike. Against this even-handedness, communalism (whether Hindu, Muslim, or any other) seeks special privileges for non-negotiable, exclusivist religious-cultural identities. Hindu communalism's specific mode of attack on state secularism is to call it 'pseudo-secularism', and to accuse it of 'pampering minorities' and denying Hindus the dominant status they ought to have in India. Unlike the Nehruvian era, when the exclusionary effects of the dominant model of nationalism were unseen and certainly unemphasized, Hindu communalism is founded on the explicit and insistent exclusion of those defined as 'others', specially Muslims, and lately also Christians. Where the Nehruvian spatial metaphor of the steel plant or the hydroelectric project was unable or unwilling to accord much importance to cultural distinctions, hindutva's new spatial metaphors are designed to serve precisely as markers of irreducible cultural difference.

Why has hindutva rejuvenated itself during the 1980s and 1990s in particular? Part of the negative side of the explanation, as suggested in the previous section, is to be found in the erosion of the foundations of Nehruvianism. Perhaps one of the reasons on the positive side has to do with the rapid expansion of the communications network. Initially established as part of the Nehruvian scheme to spread the message of national development, radio and specially television have undergone radical changes in the decades since Nehru. The dramatic expansion of television broadcasting in the 1980s (with the 1982 Asian Games held in Delhi as the springboard) created—for the first time in Indian history—a national network organized around a medium more

powerful than either print or radio.[15] Special mention must be made
of the historic role played by the *Ramayana* teleserial in preparing
fertile ground for the emergence of hindutva. While its impact was
largely unforeseen and unintended, this teleserial and its subsequent
imitators were instrumental in inviting a vast, hitherto un-addressed,
audience to rediscover their 'stories-in-common', stories that hindutva
could use as a springboard.[16]

Against this background, there are at least three distinct kinds of
spatial strategies that hindutva has employed in our recent history,
those centred on places, areas, and routes.

PLACES OF ESSENCE: SACRED SITES

The strategy based on the site has two facets. First, a chosen spot or site
is invested with some unique particularity, such that it can be declared
to be the only one of its kind; or if a site already has some such claims,
these claims are refined and amplified. However—and this is the
second aspect of the strategy—the criterion of selection is that the spot
must implicate the 'other' deeply enough to prevent easy extrication.
The combined result is to prepare a battleground where Hindu 'pride'
or 'self-respect' can be defended only by inflicting an insult of some
kind on the 'other'. This inexorably zero-sum logic (my victory must
mean your defeat) is designed to position hindutva in a win-win
position vis-à-vis its (usually Muslim) enemy: if they surrender the
site in question, victory is declared and celebrated as the defeat of the
Muslim; if they don't, this is treated as evidence of Muslim fanaticism,
and used as a justification for escalating the conflict.

The most successful example of the site-based strategy is, of course,
the campaign for the 'liberation' of the Babri Masjid-Ram
Janmabhoomi in Ayodhya. The transformation of this rural small
town from merely another geographically specific place into a powerful
symbol was the result of a conscious spatial strategy—there was
nothing 'natural' about it. Although historically several other places
have claimed the name, it seems reasonable to assume that this

particular Ayodhya has always been roughly where it is today. It has been known for several centuries as the supposed birthplace of Lord Rama, one of the principal deities of the Hindu pantheon. That a Hindu temple was supposed to have been destroyed here by a general representing a Muslim emperor—this too has been known for more than four and a half centuries. Thus the 'natural endowments' of Ayodhya as a particular physical place have been the same for quite some time; but its successful incorporation in the spatial strategies of hindutva is a very recent occurrence.

This has been effected by, first, devaluing, suppressing or simply disowning all other versions of the Ram legend, and declaring this particular place and this specific site to be the one-and-only birthplace of Ram. As a unique (and uniquely holy) spot, the Janmabhoomi is invested with a sacred essence that is presented as being beyond all discussion or negotiation, beyond even the law of the land. Secondly, it is not by accident that the site designated as *the* birthplace of Ram is also the site of a masjid—the objective of this strategy is to require the destruction of the masjid in order that 'Hindu sentiment' be respected, particularly since it is alleged to have been built after the destruction of a temple four and a half centuries ago. The whole point is to construct a site of confrontation where faith meets faith in a fight to the finish. The Janmabhoomi controversy (and the numberless mosques/ temples in Kashi, Mathura and elsewhere that are said to be awaiting liberation) emerge as answers to the question: where (and how) can temple-construction be made indistinguishable from mosque-demolition?

It is pertinent to note, however, that construction has always been subordinated to demolition within this implacable I-win-you-lose logic. The popular slogan of the BJP-VHP movement, which its leaders (specially the hardliners like Vinay Katiyar, Murli Manohar Joshi or Sadhavi Rithambhara) were getting crowds to repeat at public meetings—'Mandir *wahin* banayenge'—always had its characteristic emphasis on the middle word. ('We're going to build a temple *right there*'.) In a context where several compromise solutions for building a temple without demolishing the mosque were being discussed, this adamant insistence on that very spot was a pivotal aspect of the hindutva campaign. It was precisely such an 'unreasonable' insistence on those few square metres of land being the exact birthplace of Ram hundreds and thousands of years ago—this refusal to budge 'even one inch'— that was worn as a badge of honour by the movement.

The success of the site-based strategy at Ayodhya was based on strengthening the link between a concrete place and the abstract, utopian space of hindutva; and second, on the forging of a bond between this utopia and the people for whom it provides a renewed sense of belonging. Although it exploited religious feelings, there was nothing religious about the strategy itself—it may be readily analysed like any other political strategy. Just to illustrate this point, and to see what happens when the same strategy is deployed without easy access to religious notions of the sacred, it may be useful to consider another example, that of the Idgah Maidan flag hoisting controversy at Hubli, a city in northern Karnataka, about 100 km south of the Maharashtra border, with a population of about seven lakh. During the last decade, Hubli has earned a place on the national map of communal violence, with Hindu-Muslim 'riots' taking place almost every year; it also happens to be my home town.

The Idgah Maidan is a roughly triangular piece of land about half the size of a football field in what has now become central or 'downtown' Hubli. In 1922, it was located on the outskirts of the city, and the British municipal administration gave it on a long-term lease at a nominal rent of one rupee per annum to a Muslim cultural organization, the *Anjuman-e-Islam*, Hubli. However, local history suggests that the lease merely formalized what was established usage, the area having been associated with Muslim organizations and activities (including specially the Id prayers) for about two centuries or more. During the 1970s, with the real estate value of the land having increased dramatically, the Anjuman's attempt to build a school-cum-commercial complex on one part of the plot was challenged in court by 'public spirited individuals', and a stay order has been in force, the matter being currently in the Supreme Court.

Against this background, attempts were begun in the 1990s by Hindu communal interests to recruit this issue for the hindutva campaign. Partly inspired by the example of Murli Manohar Joshi's symbolic hoisting of the Indian tricolour in Srinagar, the local affiliates, and allies of the VHP, RSS, BJP and Shiv Sena formed front organizations (such as the Rashtra Dhwaja Gaurava Samrakshana Samiti—or Society to Defend the Honour of the National Flag) and launched an agitation demanding the right to hoist the national flag at the Idgah Maidan on Independence Day and Republic Day. Since the unconcealed intent of this agitation was to undermine the Anjuman's right to the land, the organization refused to allow the flag hoisting. Largely because of their fear of law and order problems, the courts, too, have consistently refused permission to hoist the flag on the maidan. The mass campaign by the hindutva organizations to hoist the flag in defiance of court orders has resulted in mob violence, repeated imposition of curfew, and police actions including firings in which at least five persons have died and dozens have been injured since 1993.[17]

In terms of the present argument, therefore, the Idgah Maidan campaign represents a variation on the Ayodhya strategy. It attempts to shift from a religious to a secular-nationalist idiom of contestation, from Ram to the flag. But the overall logic is the same: an unreasonable insistence on a particular site; the blocking of all negotiations and compromises; and a systematic effort to trap the adversary in a lose-lose situation—allow flag hoisting and risk losing the land, or disallow it and jeopardize your nationalist credentials. However, it is the *differences* between Ayodhya and Hubli that are instructive, specially in their ability to illuminate the process by which a particular site is more or less suitable for the spatial strategies of hindutva. While it is situated within the overall framework of hindutva, the Idgah Maidan campaign depended on two specific types of shared experiences. One is the concrete, experiential recognition of the Maidan as a *public* space, and the other is the *visual-symbolic* impact of its location.

The open space that comprises the Idgah Maidan has always been used as public space. I remember it from my childhood as the parking space for the carts and bullocks of vegetable farmers from the nearby villages; light trucks and tractor trailers have joined them in the last ten to fifteen years. There have always been the immoveable groups of cattle and the vendors commonly found in such places, selling everything from cucumbers to combs. One corner of the Maidan has long been used as a public urinal. On any given day, the centre might be occupied by women offering cheap meals for the poor; rope-makers braiding long strands of coir, twine or nylon; or, occasionally, a small travelling amusement park for children with a giant wheel, swings and merry-go-round.

The point is that such a massive accumulation of popular memory of the Maidan as a 'non-exclusive' public space (except for the two days in the year that Id prayers are offered) provides strong support for the hindutva strategy of questioning 'Muslim' rights to the land. The success of this strategy depends on ignoring the countless other instances of encroachment of public space by all sorts of commercial establishments, individuals and groups that can be observed within walking distance of the Maidan. 'Muslims pampered by the government' can thus be made to bear the burden of the genuine frustration and anger that people feel at the vanishing of urban commons and open spaces.

The other crucial aspect—and this is perhaps what precipitated the issue in the first place—is the visual affront to the hindutva sensibility of a large and imposing 'Muslim' building on the Maidan. For it was in 1972 that the Maidan first became controversial, with the launching of a successful public interest litigation against the Anjuman's plan to build a school-cum-commercial complex at one end of the Maidan (Karnataka High Court 1983:6). In order to appreciate this point it is necessary to understand the contemporary location of the Maidan in the social field of vision.

With the growth and development of the city, the Idgah Maidan now occupies the very heart of the city, adjacent to Traffic Island, which is the arterial junction of the main streets that lead on to highways headed for Bangalore, Hyderabad, and Pune/Bombay. In the centre of the roundabout is a large equestrian statue of Rani Channamma, celebrated martyr of armed resistance to the British. (The regent/queen of Kittur, a small principality nearby, she is to Karnataka what the Rani of Jhansi is to north India.) Along the base of this plot of land, which resembles a triangle with its apex lopped off, is a large shopping complex dominated by the biggest of the many Kamat restaurants in the city. (Incidentally, this well known chain and its founder, Rangappa Kamat, began their careers in Hubli, which is still the business's headquarters.) Along one side of the triangle are a series of new multi-storeyed commercial complexes housing the offices of multinational and large Indian firms, upscale shops and arcades. Along the other are the local courts, the office of the Assistant Commissioner of Police, and the offices of the Hubli-Dharwad Municipal Corporation are round the corner.[18]

Given the centrality—in every sense of the word—of the Idgah Maidan, the prospect of a prominent visual mark of Muslim presence (in the form of the proposed building) could not be entertained within the hindutva world view. The flag hoisting campaign was the logical extension of the drive to contain, and if possible erase, this sign of Muslim presence in the heart of the city, sharing social space with all the other visual markers of (Hindu) power, wealth and domination. Such antipathy to the visual markers of Muslim presence—specially if they seem assertive, prosperous, or more generally, fail to display marks of subordination—are not unusual in a communalized society.[19] Once again, this is not a situation unique to Hubli, but is common to the numerous Indian cities and towns with significant Muslim populations.

While these two features, (namely the displaced anger of the urban middle classes at the shrinking of public spaces, and the fear that the visual hierarchies proper to a Hindu-dominated social space might be upset), enabled the recruitment of the Idgah Maidan for a site-based spatial strategy, perhaps they also restricted its scope and strength in comparison to Ayodhya. A probable explanation is that, first, the Maidan's claim to being a site of unique essence was much weaker—it was not obvious why the national flag needed to be hoisted on that specific spot. Second, this essence (resentment at Muslim 'visibility') was not abstract—and therefore 'portable'—enough. Although it was provoked by fears and frustrations common to other locations, the Maidan campaign had no effective way of projecting these shared experiences, and worked well only with those with some first-hand experience of the site. As an essence, 'the birthplace of Ram' was powerful and abstract enough to attract huge numbers of kar sevaks who had never been to Ayodhya before. However, the demand to hoist the national flag at the Idgah Maidan, though designed to achieve the same broad objectives as the Ayodhya campaign, could not sustain for long the commitment of armies of outsiders who did not have a personal experience of the 'meaning' of Idgah Maidan. Of course, the manifest cynicism and hypocrisy of such a demand emanating from organizations (like the RSS) which themselves have refused to recognize or respect the national flag in the past, may also have helped discredit the campaign.

It is in this sense that the less successful instance of the site-based strategy offers a better view of its mechanisms. Perhaps the Hubli campaign erred in opting for a site-based strategy rather than a more modest neighbourhood-based one; or perhaps it simply illustrates the relative ideological efficacy of religious and national symbols today.

AREAS OF INTIMACY: LOCALITIES AND NEIGHBOURHOODS

Unlike the site-based strategy which involves an abstract, universal essence embedded in the site, the spatial strategy based on the *neighbourhood* emphasizes the concrete intimacy that everyday familiarity with a given locale makes possible. The status of Ayodhya as site-of-essence (*the* birthplace of Ram) is an abstract and universal one; its sacredness is intended to address all Hindus equally—those who happen to reside in Ayodhya are not necessarily privileged over those living elsewhere. (Indeed it is precisely because of this universalized relationship that armies of the faithful who are themselves from elsewhere can invade the site to 'reclaim' it.) Moreover, site-based campaigns necessarily acquire an occasion-specific, do-or-die character that is the very antithesis of the quotidian. They take the form of heroic struggles conducted in short spasms of 'revolutionary' or 'sacred' time, during which the profane logic of everyday life is swept aside, albeit temporarily.

By contrast, spatial strategies based on the neighbourhood build on the sedimented banalities of 'neighbourliness'—the long-term, 'live-in' intimacy of residential relationships among persons and families, and between them and their local environment. Such strategies are at home in the *longue durée* of the quotidian, and seek to recruit mundane, everyday experiences for the cause. The ideological forms of address that they typically employ are designed to hail those who inhabit the space that is to be incorporated into a spatial strategy.

Contemporary Hindu communalism and its embeddedness in neighbourhoods seems to involve the intersection of notions of cultural kinship ('our people') and residential belonging ('our area').[20] This is obviously related to the fact that the major communal organizations have all tried (in different styles and with varying degrees of emphasis) to leverage their cause on the fulcrum of the *family*, an institution defined more than any other by the interlocking ties of blood and residence. However, a more detailed study of this aspect of communalism may help to clarify the ways in which the patterns of both kinship relations and human settlements are not *given* as 'primordial' categories, but are painstakingly *constructed* and reconstructed, even though this construction is subject to definite limitations.

The Bombay-based Shiv Sena, for example, has established itself by seeking the involvement of not just individuals but their entire families.[21] This emphasis has blended very well with the Sena's reliance on neighbourhood-level organization through its shakhas and *gata-shakhas* (sub-shakhas). As a result, middle and lower level

Sena functionaries like the shakha and gata pramukhs are solidly entrenched in lower middle class and poorer neighbourhoods. As people who deal with everyday local issues ranging from 'husband-wife problems to leaking pipes', they are people with strong local roots and are well known to the residents of their neighbourhoods.[22]

The full implications of the neighbourhood as the basis for a spatial strategy emerge in the context of their actual mobilization for some larger-than-everyday activity or campaign, often related to or resulting in communal violence. The Shiv Sena and RSS sponsored 'maha-arti' has emerged as an important example in the context of the countrywide spell of anti-Muslim violence following the destruction of the Babri Masjid in December 1992. While both organizations have been involved in reinventing and politicizing Hindu festivals, the maha-arti is a recent development designed to 'recapture the streets for Hindus'.[23] It is said to have had a direct role in the instigation of violence against Muslims in Bombay, and in the widening of the support base for such violence in middle-class localities (Sharma 1995:283; Heuze 1995:242). Also relevant in this context is the neighbourhood-based organization of what might be called 'exchange violence'. This involves an explicitly planned strategy whereby the residents of neighbourhood A will, in connivance with the Hindus of neighbourhood B, attack the Muslims of the latter locality in return for similar attacks on Muslims in their own locality by the Hindus of neighbourhood B.[24] Occupying the other end of the spectrum, but also based on the locality, is the phenomenon of violence born of contiguity, where members of the majority practise 'ethnic cleansing' against their own minority-community neighbours.[25]

While it is broadly true to say that

> popular vision centred on space is usually both defensive and decentralized. The street, or a small part of the street, sometimes the slum or the mohalla, are the common notions of popular space (Heuze 1995:244),

such a view underestimates the extent to which this apparent limitation can be converted into a source of strength. In the last analysis, the significance of the locality as a spatial strategy is not really in terms of what it is able to achieve within its own spatial limits, but rather in the possibilities it creates for inserting such localities into a larger grid of ideological dissemination and political action. Thus, the neighbourhood acts as a sort of relay which, though it is crucially dependent on its particular location in social space, can nevertheless provide the ideological context for the production and reproduction of world views, as well as properly indoctrinated workers for the hindutva cause. Localities and neighbourhoods form part of the conditions of possibility for the spatial strategies based on the site and the route. Simply put, these everyday spaces supply the (usually lower class and lower caste) crowds recruited for the campaigns of/for hindutva—they are the neighbourhoods from where the crowds come, and to which they return.

ROUTES OF SYNERGY: PROCESSIONS AND PILGRIMAGES

Spatial strategies based on pilgrimages and processions bring together and set in motion the adamantly zero-sum logic produced by sites-of-essence and the masses of committed agents provided by areas-of-intimacy. The forte of such strategies is thus their *dynamism*, which serves to vastly amplify the political-ideological impact of hindutva.

The pilgrimage has been an integral part of the world of the faithful since ancient times, and may always have involved questions of hegemony, power and territorial control. Its redeployment as an explicitly political spatial strategy involving a ritualized mass-journey is also well known in recent history, as shown by the widely different examples of Mao Zedong (the 'Long March'), Mahatma Gandhi (Dandi March) and Martin Luther King (the March to Montgomery). But its repeated and effective use in current Indian politics has been a characteristic of the Sangha Parivar, the loosely linked set of organizations under the umbrella of the RSS.

The first of these political pilgrimages was the *ekatmata yajna* organized by the Vishwa Hindu Parishad (VHP) in 1983, which comprised three main *yatras* criss-crossing the country from Hardwar to Kanyakumari, Kathmandu to Rameshwaram and Gangasagar to Somnath. With its forty-seven subsidiary yatras, this 'yajna' claimed to have reached 60 million people in India, not to speak of the international participation from Hindu communities in Nepal, Bhutan, Myanmar, Bangladesh, Pakistan and Mauritius, who sent 'holy water' from their local rivers. The yajna and its cross-country processions 'garnered enormous publicity and enabled the VHP to start local branches in all parts of the country' (Van der Veer 1996:124-26). This was followed, of course, by the much more overtly politicized yatras—Advani's *rathayatra* to Ayodhya, which dragged a trail of communal violence in its wake; Joshi's Kanyakumari to Kashmir yatra culminating in the farcical hoisting of the national flag in Srinagar; the less successful 'jan aadesh' yatra; and most recently, Narendra Modi's 'Gaurav Yatra' in Gujarat. As the last example has shown, this strategy is now beginning to look more and more like the electoral stunt that it has become.

A more frequently used and much more powerful spatial strategy is that based on a localized mass-procession. Usually operating on a city-wide scale, the procession exemplifies the synergistic fusion of both the site and neighbourhood based strategies. The inflexible stand on the site is reproduced in the refusal to negotiate the route or destination of the procession, which is chosen with political objectives in mind; and neighbourhood based groups act as the mass base providing the well-prepared crowds which will actually form the procession. And unlike the everyday routine of neighbourhood groups or the episodic nature of site-based campaigns, the procession can be both institutionally regularized and more or less predictable while also providing a theatre for intensely concentrated, 'spontaneous' outbursts of political energy, often leading to violence. In the procession, both the site-based and the neighbourhood-based strategies can hope to overcome their limitations: the former can become more flexible and regulated, while the latter can transcend its local ambit and become mobile.

As part of her larger project on the new predicaments facing old cities, the sociologist, Ratna Naidu has conducted what is perhaps the most detailed study of its kind, mapping the evolution and the spatial-political impact of processions in the city of Hyderabad (Naidu 1992). The city has three traditional processions associated with religious festivals: the *Ganesh Utsav* procession dates from the turn of the century; the *Bibi ka Alam julus*, part of Muharram, the Muslim festival of mourning, originates in the Qutub Shahi period (1591-1687); and the *Bonalu* festival procession, involving incarnations of Kali worshipped by lower-caste Hindus (with mostly women processionists), is by far the oldest as it is associated with the indigenous population of the area. However, the use of processions as political devices is very recent, having begun only in the late 1970s.

Since the 1980s, the major Hindu (i.e., the Ganesh and Bonalu) processions have changed dramatically in size and character. They have become incomparably larger, in terms of the number of 'tributary' processions, the length of the routes and the numbers of processionists. (For example, the 1984 Ganesh procession involved no less than 151 sub-processions which joined around Charminar to form one mammoth procession, and then proceeded through the centre of the city to the Husain Sagar lake—renamed Vinayak Sagar for the day!—about 8 km away. And the Bonalu procession of the same year involved thirty-five subsidiaries.) The changes in size are also related to the change in the nature of processions. From small, local religious-cultural events they have now become prominent political theatres for demonstrating strength and exerting aggressive pressure on opponents, particularly the Muslim community. Thus, routes have been changed to pass through Muslim localities and by major mosques, ensuring that the potential for provocation is maximized.[26]

A new *Pankha procession* seems to have been launched by Muslim communal organizations during the 1980s in response to the provocations of the reorganized Ganesh and Bonalu processions, and has also resulted in violent conflicts. But the institutionalized and vastly superior ability of the Hindu processions to generate violence is reflected in the way that respondents have answered the survey questions on this subject.[27] 80 per cent of the Muslim respondents emphatically support a government ban on all processions, while the figure for both Hindus and Scheduled Castes/Tribes is 53 per cent. 29 per cent of Hindus and 22 per cent of the Scheduled Caste/Tribe respondents oppose a ban on the ground that it would restrict religious freedom, while the figure for Muslims—commonly projected as religious fanatics—is only 8 per cent. Perhaps the most telling figures are those on participation in processions: a mere 6 per cent of Muslims say that they participate in the processions organized by their community, compared to 32 per cent of Hindus and 49 per cent of the SC/STs. (Naidu 1990:135, Table 7.5.)

Hyderabad is not an exception—the systematic use of processions by Hindu communalists has long been an established feature of the Indian political scene. The reports of several commissions of inquiry, set up to look into incidents of communal violence, provide a depressingly detailed testimony on their repeated and varied use all over India, and specially in the north. Thus, for example, the Justice D.P. Madon Committee Report traces the history of the Shiv Jayanti procession (which commemorates Shivaji's birthday—strictly speaking, not a religious festival) in Bhiwandi over four successive years, describing in minute detail the fashioning of the procession into an incendiary device (Madon 1974). And, as if to prove that the procession-based strategy is an abstract conceptual scheme immune to particularities, the Justice Jaganmohan Reddy Committee Report records the circumstances in which a 'procession' of cows was instrumental in igniting the notorious Ahmedabad riots of 1969 (Reddy 1970).[28]

As a spectacular and often terrifying demonstration of strength, the spatial strategy based on the procession is in a class of its own. It offers the cover of large numbers and a semi-religious occasion for premeditated attacks on the person and property of adversaries. At the same time, as an institutionalized and regular annual event, it tacitly offers hospitality and encouragement for semi-planned or unplanned 'spontaneous' violence that can then be disowned by the larger organizations responsible for the procession. If neighbourhood-based strategies can sometimes be defensive, the procession is unmistakably offensive in orientation.

Conclusion: The Roads Not Taken

In this chapter and the previous one, I have tried to outline two of the major styles in which the Indian nation has been imagined in recent times. But this remains a partial analysis that needs to be complemented in several ways. For communalism or economism are not the only forces attempting to reshape the nation: several others are also at work, and it is the *net effect* that will be decisive.

Of these other forces, five seem to be crucial: the New Economic Policy in place since 1991; the range of processes loosely termed 'globalization'; the resurgence of caste issues; the emergence of the 'new middle classes' and their changed role; and, as the combined effect of the first four, a new regionalization of the Indian nation. The following chapters will consider some of these factors from different vantage points.

CHAPTER FIVE

Caste Inequalities in India Today

Seen from the vantage point of the Nehruvian era, the 1980s and 1990s have witnessed what psychoanalysts call 'the return of the repressed'—the reappearance in pathological form of unresolved tensions censored from conscious memory. One such problem, Hindu communalism, was discussed in the last chapter on the spatial strategies of *Hindutva*, caste is another. In a way, the resurgence of the caste question—more specifically, the renewed militancy and social visibility of the so-called lower castes—has been much more of a shock to the largely upper-caste urban middle classes than the revival of hindutva.

During the Nehruvian era, the national consensus on caste seemed much more comprehensive and durable than the one on secularism. Caste—unlike religion—was among the few 'traditional' institutions that were presented as all bad, as 'social evils' without any redeeming features. It was as if the only civilized response to caste was to urge its abolition. And in the 1950s and '60s it seemed as though everyone was civilized, for no one argued otherwise. To the generations born in Nehruvian India, and specially to those who (like me) were brought up in a traditionally upper-caste but newly urban and newly professional middle-class environment, caste was an archaic concept. True, it would be brought out of figurative mothballs to preside over traditional rites of passage, specially marriage, but it seemed to have no active role in urban everyday life.

It is only now—after Mandal, so to speak—that we are beginning to understand why caste was almost invisible in urban middle-class contexts. The most important reason, of course, is that these contexts were overwhelmingly dominated by the upper castes. This homogeneity made caste drop below the threshold of social visibility. If almost everyone around is upper-caste, caste identity is unlikely to be an issue, just as our identity as 'Indians' may be relevant abroad but goes unnoticed in India. Moreover, it was precisely the upper castes who had the least problems in supporting the official and social-moral ban on public discussion of caste in the decades after Independence. Whatever their personal views on the subject, it is reasonable to suppose that as a social group that benefitted from the system, the upper castes would not have been averse to the absence of public debate on caste.

Despite its status as the discipline most concerned with the subject, Indian sociology seems to have done little to account for or to counter the tendency for caste to vanish from view in precisely those contexts where it had been most effective. This chapter attempts, therefore, to pin down a strong yet oddly elusive uneasiness that I have felt about the *partial*—that is to say, incomplete, and therefore also biased— understanding of caste in Indian sociology.[1]

I first recognized this uneasiness for what it was at a crowded upper middle-class Chinese restaurant in Secunderabad. The restaurant was just 'upper' enough to play reggae music and to require that diners wait to be seated, but also 'middle' enough to serve saunf and sugar with the bill. Furious because he felt others had been seated ahead of his own group, a plump middle-aged man in a safari suit was berating the manager in authoritative Indian English. Although he was yelling, I would not have noticed his voice in the general din but for the incongruous northern accent. 'Are we *scheduledcastes* or what?' he shouted.

The phrase 'Scheduled Castes' sounds appropriately quaint in Anglo-American English, specially if one recounts its colonial origins in the Government of India Act of 1935, which required the preparation of Schedules listing the castes and tribes forming the 'Depressed Classes'. But as is well known, the phrase is used as a single word in Indian English, a common noun without capitals, and that is how the man used it. And everyone understood him perfectly well—the hapless manager, the rival group that he suspected of usurping his table, his own companions, even bystanders like myself.

What made me uneasy was my gut feeling that being a sociologist had placed me at a *disadvantage* vis-à-vis the other bystanders in interpreting this incident. My discipline did not offer much help in figuring out what caste means in places like a big-city Chinese restaurant, or for people who wear safari suits. Instead, it pointed me towards villages, religious beliefs about purity and pollution, ritual rules and customs about food and marriage . . . I do not mean to suggest that these are the wrong directions—far from it. But these are not the *only*—or perhaps even the most crucial—locations where caste has been flourishing in independent India, unmindful of its legal abolition half a century ago.

A popular series of advertisements asks us to think of a particular paint company whenever we see colour; whenever we think of caste, Indian sociology seems to invite us to 'see' villages, rituals, rites and so on. This is a true but partial view that risks becoming untrue because it is unaware (or insufficiently aware) of its partiality. It is of this risk that the safari-suited gentleman reminds us by demonstrating that caste is alive and kicking in the urban middle-class, and has had a thoroughly modern makeover. He may no longer remember caste names or care about the caste of the cooks in the restaurant, he may never have set foot in a village. But Mr Safari Suit knows who *'scheduledcastes'* are, how they are to be treated, and why people like himself are infinitely superior—in short, he knows everything a 'user' needs to know about caste.

Caste as seen from sociology: what is missing?

Today, a decade after the bitter controversy over the Mandal

Commission report, we may be better placed to appreciate the irony in the fact that this controversy offered us—albeit by accident—a rare window of insight into Indian sociology. Given the centrality of caste, an undeniably 'sociological' subject, one would normally have expected the discipline to shed light on the controversy rather than the other way around. Of course, such expectations were not entirely belied. But while some sociologists did gain rare public attention for their comments, the discipline itself gained little in prestige and authority.

This was not because sociologists adopted unpopular stances. In fact, the most prominent among them were vocal in their support for the anti-Mandal position which dominated urban middle-class perceptions of this issue and received wide and strongly sympathetic coverage in the metropolitan media. But, by and large, sociologists were unable to say anything that went beyond popular commonsense.

In this respect they were no different from the journalists, politicians, administrators, other academics or legions of self-proclaimed pundits commenting on the subject. Like everyone else, sociologists too concentrated on the *possible consequences of implementing the Mandal Report.* Forgotten were the questions that ought to have come first, at least for a discipline claiming specialized knowledge of caste as a social institution: *Is caste discrimination still practised in contemporary India? Does it continue to breed inequality? What is the nature and extent of such inequality today? How has it been changing since independence?*

It may seem painfully obvious that problems must be discussed before solutions are debated, but exactly the opposite seems to have happened during the Mandal controversy. What is most remarkable, however, is that sociologists should have shared in and helped accentuate such a perverse response. By addressing crucial questions which the overnight experts were unable to answer, sociologists could have demonstrated that their discipline provides insights that commonsense cannot. But it seems in retrospect that the sociologists' silence on questions of caste inequality was not so much perverse as prudent. As a matter of fact, despite all its claims to an expertise on caste, Indian sociology did not have the answers, never having shown much interest in macro-analyses of caste inequality. The important point, though, is that this lack of interest was itself invisible because it was so much a part of business as usual in Indian sociology.[2] It took a national crisis as big as Mandal to alert us to this blind spot, and to goad us into recognizing it as a problem. But let me backtrack a bit to clarify precisely what the Mandal controversy revealed about Indian sociology.

UNEQUAL INEQUALITIES

In its incarnation as *hierarchy,* the idea of inequality is hardly absent from the sociology of India, since it is at the heart of the classic models of the caste system. But the hierarchy avatar of inequality is rather different from the sort of inequality that was at issue in the Mandal controversy. In fact, one could even say that the two are incommensurable.

To begin with, the notion of hierarchy implicated in the caste system tends to *relativize inequality.* While it is obvious that you cannot have hierarchy without inequality, social anthropological models of caste stress the systemic nature of this inequality: almost everyone in the system is unequal with respect to almost everyone else, being above some groups and below others. Because everybody is unequal, they are also in a certain sense equalized by this fact. For instance, in the most sophisticated theoretical model of the caste system we have, that of Louis Dumont, the key feature is the subordination of the (Kshatriya) king to the (Brahmin) priest. This means that even the highest secular power (the king) requires religious sanction from the priest; and even the caste with the highest ritual rank (Brahmin) is subject to the secular power of a caste of lower rank. Thus, the anthropological understanding of caste as hierarchy blunts the sharp edge that inequality often acquires in other contexts.

This is reinforced by the fact that caste in anthropology is defined as essentially a *consensual system based on complementarity*—this is what differentiates castes from ethnic groups, for example. All castes in a caste system recognize the same basic hierarchy and accept (or at least tacitly acknowledge) their own position within it, though there may be variations and disputes. On the other hand, every ethnic group can have its own version of a social hierarchy in which it usually places itself at the top. Moreover, one ethnic group is conceptually and functionally the same as any other group, whereas castes are functionally differentiated and complement each other, the most obvious illustration of this being the well-known occupational specialization or division-of-labour version of caste. Of course, this describes the classical and not the contemporary anthropological understanding of caste, but the traditional models have cast a long shadow.[3]

More generally, influential schools of social anthropology have tended to distance caste from the material world and its political conflicts by locating it in the vicinity of religious ritual, ideology and belief systems.[4] Such a conceptualization, in turn, is both cause and consequence of an excessive emphasis on values to the exclusion of interests. Thus, much of anthropology has dealt with caste in terms of religious texts, ritual status linked to notions of purity and pollution, and rules and customs about marriage (endogamy) and food-sharing (commensality). This is indeed a far cry from the rough and tumble of competitive caste politics in independent India, specially in the Mandal era.

If proponents of Dumont's 'book' view of Indian society have severely neglected the political dimensions of caste inequality, the rival camp advocating M.N. Srinivas' 'field' view is less culpable on this count. It is a frequently mentioned matter of pride for the discipline that a sociologist, M.N. Srinivas, invented terms such as 'sanskritisation', 'dominant caste' and 'vote bank' which have come to dominate popular perceptions of the politics of caste in modern India. There can be no denying the fact that the Srinivas-inspired fieldwork of the 1960s and '70s has greatly improved our understanding of the

concrete content of caste relations and their dynamics vis-à-vis class
and power in specific regional contexts. But even this school has had
its shortcomings.

One major problem has been the almost exclusive reliance on
the standard anthropological method of intensive fieldwork by a single
scholar in a very small area (usually a single village). While this has
certainly yielded valuable insights, it has precluded any significant
attempts at developing a macro-perspective based on a more broad-
based coverage of the field. Survey methods in particular have
remained underdeveloped.[5]

But most important, perhaps, is the fact that influential sociologists
have tended to run with the hare and hunt with the hounds on this
issue. They have been the first to criticize the methods used and the
macro-data produced to track caste inequality, and their criticisms
have often been quite legitimate. However, they have also been in the
forefront of opposition to initiatives for the systematic collection of
macro-level data on caste, even though they have not, by and large,
shown any eagerness to suggest alternative methodologies for data
collection.

In the early 1990s, for example, mauling the Mandal
Commission's report for its weak database and questionable
methodology had become something of a professional pastime for
sociologists. But rarely were critics willing to specify what available
datasets the Commission had failed to utilize, precisely how it could
have improved upon its methodology, and, more generally, how it
could have done a better job within the given constraints.[6] And yet, a
few years later, when the collection of caste data in the 2001 census
was being mooted, the same voices were heard denouncing this
proposal as not just impractical but pernicious.[7] Once again there was
little concern for suggesting alternatives.

Such persistently contradictory behaviour suggests that the real
problem with researching caste inequality is not the pragmatic one of
data availability, but something deeper. Perhaps the relevant place to
look is the prevailing commonsense on caste, which shapes sociologists

and is also shaped by them.

COMMONSENSE ON CASTE INEQUALITY

It would be misleading to suggest that there is any one homogenous commonsense view of caste inequality. Nevertheless, most urban, educated, middle-class (and therefore largely upper-caste) Indians would tend to think of caste inequality in ways that would include the following elements:

1. Caste inequality is a social evil, in fact a rather terrible thing, and we have to admit that it used to be very bad in the past. However, after independence, things have been changing rapidly, even if not as swiftly or comprehensively as might be desired. The condition of the lowest castes and tribes is improving steadily; the link between caste and occupation is weakening, and members of every caste are now engaged in a much wider variety of occupations than before. Reservation has provided very real benefits to the SC/ST group, but this is being monopolized by a minority within the group. Reservation policies and the like have now become involved in the electoral arithmetic of vote banks and so are extended and continued in all sorts of contexts where they are not warranted.

2. Caste has been given a new lease of life by its encashability in politics. Backward status is now something advantageous and is fought for by all sorts of castes. Since politics is dominated by the numerically stronger lower and middle castes, the upper castes are now facing a very real reverse discrimination.

3. There is a great variation in the economic and social status of members of every caste group. This variation makes it misleading to use caste per se as a criterion to decide backwardness or forwardness. More objective criteria sensitive to individual contexts are needed. The time may have come when caste is no longer particularly useful as a criterion, economic and other criteria being more relevant. Particularly with regard to job reservations, the principle of

compensatory preferences has been overextended, and this has resulted in the 'murder of merit'.

4. Socially and culturally, the main aspect of caste discrimination, namely untouchability, has already been outlawed, and legislatively there is not much more to be done in this area. Whatever prejudices remain are due to the stubborn attitudes of a few diehards. Such attitudes should be condemned and people should be educated to transcend them, but laws cannot really change the way people think. By and large, the upper castes have given up their prejudices and moved beyond/out of caste. Ironically, today it is the lower and middle castes who are the main props for the continuance of this pernicious system.

There is much that is true in this commonsense story, but there is also much that is not: most important, perhaps, are the questions that remain unasked. For example, it is perfectly true that, by and large, when compared to the situation prevailing at independence, the condition of all social groups, including the lowest castes and tribes, has improved today. But by how much has it improved? How have the lowest castes/tribes fared in comparison to the rest of the population?

Again, it is almost a truism to say that, today, the variety of occupations and professions among all caste groups is much wider than it was fifty years ago. However, this does not change the massive social reality that the overwhelming majority of those in the 'highest' or most preferred occupations are from the upper castes, while the vast majority of those in the most menial and despised occupations belong to the lowest castes. In short, while it is indeed significant that *some* members of the lowest castes are now able to occupy very high positions, or that *many* members of high castes are being forced into menial occupations today, this does not by itself demonstrate that caste and occupational status have been delinked. We must also ask if particular *occupations* continue to be dominated by particular caste-clusters, and whether this makes for a recognizable pattern systematically linking privilege and dis-privilege to caste. In other words, the caste-composition of the privileged groups in society is a critical yardstick: as long as this continues to reflect the dominance of the upper castes, it does not matter even if the *majority* of the members of these castes are themselves poor or disprivileged. This would only demonstrate that while caste remains a necessary precondition for making it into the privileged group, it is not in itself a sufficient condition to ensure entry. One could go on in this vein, but it may be more productive to take up the question of evidence.

Caste as a determinant of life-chances in independent India

The first and most important point to be noted when considering the evidence on caste inequality is that there have been no systematic attempts to collect such evidence. Indeed, the optimism of the Nehruvian era prompted scholars and administrators to take at face value the stridently declared intention of building a caste-less society with a caste-blind state. The explicit constitutional injunction to ignore all differences of caste, creed, religion and so on has been most faithfully followed in the case of caste. Thus, except for the constitutionally sanctioned Scheduled Tribes and Castes, no official statistics have been collected on caste in independent India. Despite the fact that both language and specially religion have proved to be divisive issues sparking violent conflicts, and even though it was the British who began this exercise, the Census of India has quite rightly continued to collect information on them. But ever since independence, the Indian Census has resolutely refused to ask citizens their caste, on the ground that the new state was 'caste blind', and that previous attempts to collect such data were part of the imperial 'divide and rule' policy. So the only reliable data we have on caste is restricted to the three way classification of 'Scheduled Caste', 'Scheduled Tribe' and 'Other'. This data can only tell us about the caste of one-fourth of the population, the remaining three-fourths being lumped together in the residual term 'Other', which includes non-Hindus and persons with no caste.

The active antipathy towards caste after independence was the joint product of, first, the nationalist movement and its campaign against caste distinctions, and, second, a reaction against what were seen as deliberate colonial policies to create and sharpen divisions among the Indian people. As recent scholarship has shown, neither of these factors is simple or straightforward. First of all, it is a gross simplification to speak of 'the' nationalist movement with a singular and unequivocal position on caste. The angularities and ambivalences of the exclusively upper-caste nationalist leadership are seen even in Gandhi: easily the most visible and effective campaigner against untouchability, the Mahatma also believed that there was something to be said for the 'varna' system which divided society into a hierarchy of segments. The second factor, too, is more equivocal than it appears to be. Although it is easy to believe that a colonial power would foster institutions that produce divisions among the subject population, it is quite difficult to disentangle 'imperial invention' from 'indigenous inheritance' in the history of caste. Moreover, the motives and intentions of the colonial state were by themselves never enough to ensure the successful reproduction over centuries of so widespread a phenomenon as caste.

Whatever the merits of the antecedent causes, the post-independence backlash against caste was strong and sustained. It ensured that one of the paradoxical lessons of modern governance—that the state must measure whatever it wishes to eradicate—would not be learnt. As a result, the data that we have on caste inequality are not only meagre but also *reluctant*, so to speak, needing to be coaxed into existence, and dependent on the accidents of scholarly interest and statistical convenience. What needs to be emphasized is that unlike other comparable situations, the paucity and poor quality of these data is the result of wilful if well-intentioned neglect: we refused to collect such data because we thought we should not collect them and did not need them. However, the irony is that the end result is not very different from what might have been the case had there been a giant conspiracy to suppress evidence of caste inequality.

It is against this background that we must evaluate the many shortcomings and silences of the available data on caste inequality.

AVAILABLE EVIDENCE ON CASTE INEQUALITY

The National Sample Survey Organization (NSSO) offers the most broad-based data sets that can provide relatively direct evidence on economic inequality across caste groups. However, for the reasons already mentioned, until the year 2000, the NSSO has always restricted itself to the constitutionally sanctioned categories of the Scheduled Tribes and Castes, with everyone else being thrown together into the vast and immensely diverse residual group of 'Other'. Because it is unable to distinguish between the very different sorts of people included in it (such as the Other Backward Classes, the 'forward' castes, and non-Hindus who may or may not have a caste identity), this category is an analytical nightmare. Nevertheless, flawed as they are, the NSSO data have demonstrated that caste continues to be a major fault line of economic inequality in contemporary India.

The last phrase is particularly important. I have taken up the most recent data available precisely in order to emphasize that we are indeed speaking of contemporary times, not of the bad old days: caste is alive and well *today*, a half-century after its official abolition. In the tables below, I present data from the last quinquennial (five-yearly) 'round' of the NSSO, the 55th Round, conducted during 1999-2000. The five-yearly or 'big sample' rounds are mammoth year-long surveys involving a huge, carefully selected sample of about 1,20,000 households from 12,000 villages and urban blocks all over India. Although academics and policy makers have been concerned about the impact of some changes in the methodology of the 55th Round, there is no reason to believe that this will affect a single time-point comparison across social groups, which is what I am doing here.[8] Moreover, the 55th Round is a historic one because it is the first to provide data separately for the 'Other Backward Classes'. This allows us, for the first time since Independence, to disaggregate the 'Other' category. In conjunction with the data on religious communities published separately by the NSSO, it is also possible to construct rough 'guesstimates' of the most elusive social group in modern India in statistical terms, namely upper-caste Hindus.[9]

Details of Monthly Per capita Consumption Expenditure (MPCE) are the most basic and widely used data collected by the NSSO surveys. Since consumption expenditure is considered to be a reliable proxy for income (which is notoriously difficult to measure directly), this is the main database used to estimate poverty levels in the country. The NSSO reports typically divide the range of monthly per capita consumption expenditure (henceforth MPCE) into twelve different size-classes, and tell us what proportion of the rural and urban populations of each social group (caste or religion-based) falls in each of these classes. The twelve size-classes are much too detailed for the purposes of this discussion, so I have consolidated them into four classes: below the official Poverty Line (defined as Rs 329 per person per month for Rural India, and Rs 458 per person per month for Urban India); from the Poverty Line to the next three size-classes above—this may be called the 'above the poverty line' class; the next three size-classes above this, which can be called the 'less poor' class; and finally, the top two MPCE classes, which can be called the 'non poor'.

For someone seeking to understand caste inequality, a severe limitation of the NSSO data is that it is heavily tilted towards the poor—though this is understandable given the policy concerns it was designed to address. It is important to understand what this means in concrete terms. For example, a hypothetical family of five members with a monthly expenditure of about Rs 1,650 or less in rural India, and about Rs 2,300 or less in urban India, would be located on or just below the Poverty Line for 1999–2000. However, at the upper end of the scale, the top two MPCE classes would include all families of five with monthly expenditures of Rs 3,875 in rural India, and Rs 7,500 in urban India—*and all families that spent more*. To put this more starkly, in the following tables, a rural family of five spending Rs 3,875 per month is clubbed together with the richest rural family you can imagine, while an urban family of five spending Rs 7,500 a month is placed in the same statistical class as the Ambanis or the Tatas!

This is the reason why we are forced to use very vague grab-bag categories like 'less poor' or 'non poor' which conceal much more than they reveal. This is in part a technical problem because the rich— or even the middle classes—are such a small proportion of the population that it is difficult to ensure that they are adequately represented by standard sampling techniques designed to cover the entire nation. In fact, the NSSO has been making special efforts to 'oversample' the urban non-poor households to ensure that enough of them are covered.[10] While we cannot blame the NSSO data for doing what they were designed to do, namely, provide a detailed profile of poverty, we can and must do two things: first, remind ourselves that even in its present form the NSSO data offers plenty of evidence pointing to the continued existence of a massive caste divide in India in the twenty-first century; and second, look for more direct evidence that is able to confirm or deny the presence of caste inequality among the privileged sections of the population.

55TH ROUND DATA ON SOCIAL INEQUALITY

Table 1 shows us the division of each social group (i.e., caste or religious community) into MPCE classes for Rural India. There are four such classes as explained earlier: Rs 329 or less, which is Below the Poverty Line (BPL); Rs 329 to Rs 470, which is Above the Poverty Line (APL); Rs 470-775 which includes the next three classes of the 'Less Poor'; and finally the topmost class of 'Non Poor' which is everyone above Rs 775. Thus, the column for Scheduled Tribes shows that almost 51 per cent of the community belongs in the BPL group while less than 3 per cent is in the 'Non Poor' group. We can similarly read down the column for any group to see its class composition—the percentage of

TABLE 1

SOCIAL GROUPS STRATIFIED BY MONTHLY PER CAPITA CONSUMPTION EXPENDITURE CLASSES, RURAL INDIA, 1999-2000

MPCE Class	ST	SC	OBC	Muslim	Christian	Sikh	Other Religions	Hindu Upper Castes?	All Groups
Below Poverty Line	50.9	42.9	33.7	37.5	24.1	6.1	42.6	16.9	33.6
Rs 329 to Rs 470	30.8	34.4	35.8	34.9	27.8	20.9	28.1	32.5	33.8
Rs 470 to Rs 775	15.6	19.2	24.5	22.2	32.5	46.1	22.0	36.6	25.3
Rs 775 or More	2.7	3.4	6.1	5.5	15.6	27.0	7.2	14.0	7.3
All Classes	100.0	100.0	100.0	100.0	100.0	100.0	100.0	100.0	100.0

Note: Columns may not add up to 100 due to rounding errors. *Source*: Reports Nos.468 and 469, NSSO, September 2001.

TABLE 2

SOCIAL COMPOSITION OF MONTHLY PER CAPITA CONSUMPTION EXPENDITURE CLASSES, RURAL INDIA, 1999-2000

MPCE Class	ST	SC	OBC	Muslim	Christian	Sikh	Other Religions	Hindu Upper Castes ?	All Groups
Below Poverty Line	15.3	23.0	37.5	11.8	1.6	0.4	0.8	9.6	100.0
Rs 329 to Rs 470	9.2	18.4	39.6	10.9	1.8	1.2	0.6	18.4	100.0
Rs 470 to Rs 775	6.2	13.7	36.2	9.2	2.8	3.6	0.6	27.6	100.0
Rs 775 or More	3.7	8.4	31.1	7.9	4.6	7.4	0.7	36.3	100.0
% of 1991 Popn	10.1	18.0	37.4★	10.5	2.2	2.0	1.4	18.4★★	100.0

Note: Rows may not add up to 100 due to rounding errors. *Source*: Reports Nos.468 and 469, NSSO, September 2001.
★ = OBC figure from NSSO 55th Round, not Census; ★★ = HUC? figure obtained as residual.

TABLE 3

SOCIAL GROUPS STRATIFIED BY MONTHLY PER CAPITA CONSUMPTION EXPENDITURE CLASSES, URBAN INDIA, 1999-2000

MPCE Class	ST	SC	OBC	Muslim	Christian	Sikh	Other Religions	Hindu Upper Castes?	All Groups
Below Poverty Line	42.6	43.1	36.0	46.5	16.3	15.0	24.7	4.9	28.5
Rs 458—Rs 775	32.6	39.2	39.7	35.9	31.8	36.4	30.9	34.8	37.4
Rs 775—Rs 1,500	19.1	15.9	20.7	15.1	36.0	34.3	31.3	43.2	26.3
Rs 1,500 or more	5.7	2.0	3.7	2.5	15.9	14.4	13.0	17.1	7.8
All Classes	100.0	100.0	100.0	100.0	100.0	100.0	100.0	100.0	100.0

Note: Columns may not add up to 100 due to rounding errors. *Source*: Reports Nos.468 and 469, NSSO, September 2001.

TABLE 4

SOCIAL COMPOSITION OF MONTHLY PER CAPITA CONSUMPTION EXPENDITURE CLASSES, URBAN INDIA, 1999-2000

MPCE Class	ST	SC	OBC	Muslim	Christian	Sikh	Other Religions	Hindu Upper Castes ?	Total
Below Poverty Line	6.0	22.7	33.9	28.0	1.7	0.9	2.1	4.7	100.0
Rs 458—Rs 775	3.5	15.7	32.7	16.5	2.5	1.7	2.0	25.4	100.0
Rs 775—Rs 1,500	2.9	9.1	24.2	9.8	4.0	2.3	2.9	44.8	100.0
Rs 1,500 or more	2.9	3.8	14.6	5.5	6.0	3.3	4.0	59.8	100.0
% of 1991 Popn	2.3	12.0	31.4*	16.7	2.9	1.8	2.3	26.6**	100.0

Note: Rows may not add up to 100 due to rounding errors. *Source*: Reports Nos.468 and 469, NSSO, September 2001.
★ = OBC figure from NSSO 55th Round, not Census; ★★ = HUC? figure obtained as residual.

its population that belongs in each of the four MPCE classes. The last column provides the class composition of the population as a whole.

However, the class composition of caste groups (i.e., the percentage of each caste's population that is BPL, APL and so on) tells us only half the story. We must also ask about the caste composition of class groups—that is, of all the people who are BPL, APL and so on, what percentage belong to the ST, SC or other caste/community groups? Table 2 provides us this information. It is computed by mapping the percentage distribution of Table 1 to the population totals for each social group. These population totals, in turn, are obtained by taking the 1991 Census data on each social group (the percentage of the total population belonging to the STs, SCs and so on in the 1991 Census) and applying it to the population projection for 2000. Table 2 is organized in terms of the four rows for each MPCE class. Thus, the row for Below the Poverty Line tells us that the BPL population of rural India was composed of 15.3 per cent STs, 23.0 per cent SCs, 37.5 per cent OBCs, and so on across the row. Tables 3 and 4 provide the same data for Urban India and are organized in exactly the same way.

To establish the continued existence of sharp caste inequalities in contemporary India, we need go no further than a comparison of the four caste groups that appear on Tables 1 and 3—ST, SC, OBC and Hindu Upper Castes (HUC). (As already explained, figures for the Hindu Upper Castes are 'guesstimates' and must be treated with caution. Please see note 9 to this chapter.) In Rural India, as Table 1 shows, more than half of the ST population lives below the poverty line. This proportion is only slightly less for the SCs at about 43 per cent, and lesser still for the OBCs at about 34 per cent. However, the HUC are markedly different, with only about 17 per cent BPL. At the other end of the class spectrum, if we look at the Rs 775 and above class, there is a reverse effect: the HUCs at 14 per cent are way ahead of the STs and SCs (both around 3 per cent) and also of the OBCs at 6 per cent. In other words, the 'non poor' are a much smaller proportion of the lower-caste population and a relatively much higher proportion of the upper-caste population. The opposite is the case with the poorest or BPL class: the lower castes have a huge proportion of their population here, while the upper castes have a relatively much smaller proportion.

In urban India, as Table 3 shows, these inequalities are even more stark. Only about 5 per cent of the HUCs are BPL, while the figures for the lower castes are much higher: 43 per cent for both STs and SCs, and 36 per cent for the OBCs. Conversely, the HUCs have a much larger proportion of their population among the 'non poor' category (or those with MPCE levels of Rs 1,500 or more)—17 per cent—compared to the single digit figures of 6, 2 and 4 for the STs, SCs and OBCs, respectively.

Coming now to the question of the caste composition of the different income or MPCE classes, we see that Tables 2 and 4 confirm the grim picture presented by the previous two Tables. The general pattern is as expected in Rural India, but Table 2 tells us one important fact, namely, that in rural society, the OBCs are the only social group with a remarkably even presence in all economic classes: they constitute 30 per cent or more of each MPCE class from the BPL to the 'non poor'. As against this, the STs and SCs are under-represented among the 'non poor' and over-represented among the BPL. The opposite is the case with the HUCs—they are over-represented among the non poor and under-represented among the BPL. Thus, while arguments about rural OBCs need to be made with care, the case for continuing caste inequalities is very strong.

However, it is in urban India—the seat of genuine privilege— that the inter-caste differences are at their starkest. The most striking feature of Table 4 is the figure in its bottom right-hand corner—the HUCs constitute almost 60 per cent of the 'non poor' urban class. The urban OBCs do not resemble their rural counterparts and are much closer to the STs and SCs in profile. In fact, urban OBCs account for more than one third of the urban BPL population. Tables 2 and 4 provide us with yet another sobering fact: in the year 2000, STs, SCs, OBCs and Muslims together account for 91 per cent of the urban BPL population and 88 per cent of the rural BPL population.

Let me emphasize, in closing this discussion of the NSSO 55th Round data, that these are very significant facts. Commonsense may tell us that the lower castes are now ruling the roost, but the facts are otherwise. Despite the major phenomenon of the rural OBCs—itself a residual, unexamined category that deserves more detailed attention—caste inequality has been flourishing in rural and specially in urban India. These data are from a very large, national survey; they report proportions averaged across thousands of cases—they cannot be dismissed as being due to inter-individual differences or statistical accidents. The differences between caste groups are too strong and too stable to be artefacts. We have to make the necessary effort to transcend the commonsense view and re-examine the question of caste inequality seriously.

CASTE AND PRIVILEGE

Among the many inanities that were part of 'ragging' in my long-past days as an undergraduate was the benign one of solving riddles, with the fresher being expected to guess the 'correct' answers to set questions asked by the seniors. One of these 'riddles', asked usually at dinner time in the dining hall, went something like this: Q: Do you see an elephant in your custard? A: No, sir. Q: Why not? A: Because it is very well hidden, sir.

This, in essence, seems to be the commonsense response to the abundant evidence in our everyday lives of the strong link between social privilege and upper-caste status. It is now firmly established in contemporary commonsense that the spirit of the times not only favours the lower castes, but is also actively opposed to the upper castes. This feeling is so entrenched in the minds of the largely upper caste urban middle classes that, when confronted with the incontrovertible evidence that most enclaves of privilege are still dominated by the upper castes, they can only insist that this merely shows how cunningly anti-upper caste biases are being hidden.

Consider, for instance, the social composition of the government sector. In a country where less than 10 per cent of the workforce is in the 'organized sector'—which includes both public and private sector employment—a government job has been and continues to be among the most coveted. But as Table 5 shows, the 'lower' castes still tend to be significantly under-represented in the government sector, and particularly in its upper echelons. Thus, despite the combined quota of 22.5 per cent for the SCs and STs, only about 6 per cent (or roughly one fourth of the reserved quota) of Class I officers of the Central government are from these groups. The representation of the Other Backward Classes—the non-upper caste, non-SC/ST castes who are considered to be 'socially and educationally backward'—is even lower, at under 5 per cent.

One may quibble with these data because they are based on the Mandal Commission's initial ('ad hoc') definition of the OBCs, which required them to meet *both* the caste criterion (i.e., belonging to the 'Shudra' castes) *and* the educational backwardness criterion (neither father nor grandfather should have studied beyond primary school).[11] One may argue that the educational criterion is a rather stringent one, and that there may well be other members of the 'Shudra' castes in government employment who do not meet it. This is certainly possible, but it seems unlikely to change the numbers significantly, for other sources also confirm the broad picture conveyed by Table 5. For example, Santosh Goyal's study (Goyal 1992a) of the social composition of the Indian Administrative Service shows that, in 1985, the 'Shudra' castes account for *less than 2 per cent* of this elite cadre, in which Brahmins were 28 per cent and Kayasthas 11 per cent. Goyal's data are based purely on the caste criterion (as identified from the last names of officers in the Consolidated Civil List) and are therefore exempt from the objection that might be raised against the Mandal Commission data. However, the caste of about 21 per cent of the officers cannot be identified by her method; of these, about 10 per cent are likely to belong to the SC/ST categories (being direct recruits above the general cut-off age of twenty-six), which leaves about 11 per cent with ambiguous last names who could belong to any caste group. Even if we make the rather unrealistic assumption that *all* the unidentified officers belong to the 'Shudra' castes, this still gives a maximum possible percentage share of 12.5 per cent, which is about one-third of their share in the general population. If we make the somewhat more reasonable assumption that the unidentified officers are equally divided among the Forward, Backward and Scheduled Castes, we get a maximum 'Shudra' share of between 5-6 per cent, which is very near the Mandal Commission's estimate for the Class I services in Table 5.

TABLE 5

Representation of Scheduled Castes, Scheduled Tribes and Other Backward Classes in Central Government Services, 1979–80

(percentage shares in class totals)

	CLASS I		CLASS II		CLASS III & IV		ALL CLASSES	
	SC/ST	OBC	SC/ST	OBC	SC/ST	OBC	SC/ST	OBC
Ministries and Departments	7.2	2.6	13.7	4.0	31.0	8.4	16.8	4.8
Autonomous Bodies, Subordinate Offices	6.6	5.1	18.2	11.7	20.8	21.0	18.1	14.4
Public Sector Undertakings	4.5	4.6	18.7	9.9	31.7	15.8	20.0	10.6
TOTAL	5.7	4.7	18.2	10.6	24.4	19.0	18.7	12.6

Source: Second Backward Classes (Mandal) Commission Report, Appendix VIII, Statement 1.

It has to be reiterated that the messiness and uncertainties that plague this data are the product of deliberate decisions. In fact, the government refuses, except under duress from statutory bodies like the SC-ST Commissions, to publish even the data relating to these constitutionally recognized categories. As Santosh Goyal points out, it is impossible to estimate accurately the aggregate numbers of SC-ST officers in the IAS because the Home Ministry does not release this data, so that there is no authoritative source of information on whether or not the reserved quotas are being filled. All the indications are that there has been a significant carried forward backlog of unfilled reserved posts during the 1970s and '80s , specially for the Scheduled Tribes (Goyal 1992a:426-27). As already seen, the situation with regard to the Other Backward Classes is much worse, with hardly any reliable data available.

TABLE 6
Caste Composition of Top Corporate Officers, 1979-80

Castes	Chairman, President	Managing Director	General Manager	Director, Ex. Director	TOTAL
Brahmin	135 (36.0)	144 (35.2)	408 (46.2)	171 (41.3)	858 (41.2)
Vaishya	83 (22.0)	103 (25.1)	122 (13.8)	64 (15.5)	372 (17.9)
'Shudra'	6 (1.6)	24 (5.9)	35 (4.0)	22 (5.3)	87 (4.2)
Lingayat	1 (0.3)	4 (1.0)	7 (0.8)	1 (0.2)	13 (0.6)
Mallick	1 (0.3)	0 (0.0)	1 (0.1)	1 (0.2)	3 (0.1)
Singh	8 (2.1)	6 (1.5)	11 (1.2)	12 (2.9)	37 (1.8)
Khatri	70 (18.7)	69 (16.8)	165 (18.7)	81 (19.6)	385 (18.5)
Kayasth	26 (6.9)	35 (8.5)	119 (13.5)	47 (11.4)	227 (10.9)
Marwari	45 (12.0)	25 (6.1)	15 (1.7)	15 (3.6)	100 (4.8)
Total Caste Identified	375 (100.0)	410 (100.0)	883 (100.0)	414(100.0)	2082(100.0)
Total Caste Unidentified	168	274	380	225	1047
Grand Total of Employees	543	684	1263	639	3129

Source: Santosh Goyal, 1990, p.540, Table IV.5 (Figs. in parentheses () are % of Total Caste Identified.

If this is the case with the government itself, one can hardly expect the corporate sector to be different. Santosh Goyal's valiant attempt (Goyal 1992b) to profile the social composition of this sector is reported in Table 6. The data in this table cover 3,129 officers of 1,100 large companies (in both the private and public sectors) that accounted for over 90 per cent of the turnover of the Indian corporate sector as a whole in 1979-80. The designations considered are the topmost in the corporate hierarchy — Chairman/President, Managing Director, General Manager and Director/Executive Director. The caste of the officers is ascertained by the last name (comparing them to the lists published in the 1931 Census, and also by consulting scholars from different regions around the country). The castes of approximately two-thirds (66.5 per cent) of the employees is ascertainable by this method, while the remaining 33.5 per cent are either non-Hindus or of unidentified castes.

As can be seen from Table 6, Brahmins are once again the dominant caste, accounting for more than 41 per cent of the total identified names, and about 27.4 per cent of all employees (including non-Hindus and Hindus of unidentified caste). They are well ahead of all other castes, the next highest being Khatris (18.5 per cent), Vaishyas (17.9 per cent) and Kayasths (10.9 per cent). In fact, these four castes together comprise almost 89 per cent of the caste-identified names. Shudras are once again very low at 4.2 per cent, while the SCs and STs are totally absent among the caste-identified names.

Apart from such formal if severely handicapped attempts to gather data on large areas of public life such as government service and corporate management, there is also a less formal or micro-level evidence that the lower castes are severely under-represented in all the modern professions. As M.N. Panini has pointed out, 'caste clustering' usually implying the overwhelming dominance of the upper castes continues to be true of professions such as engineering, medicine, banking, journalism, and academics (Panini 1996:32-36). In short, in every field offering a promising career in the contemporary world, the upper castes dominate and the middle and lower castes are more or less severely under-represented. Almost two generations after Independence, it is no longer possible to evade these realities as being the by-product of historical inequities. We have to face up to the uncomfortable truth that caste inequality has been and is being *reproduced* in independent India.

QUESTIONS OF LOCATION: SOCIOLOGY AND CASTE IN
POST-COLONIAL INDIA

It may be useful to reiterate the implications of the sort of evidence
cited above. Drastic and sustained differences in shares and proportions
averaged across very large numbers of individuals from different social
groups cannot be explained in terms of differences in individual
abilities or circumstances. As Émile Durkheim demonstrated long
ago, although every individual suicide is undoubtedly an intensely
personal event, the *average rate of suicide* in a society is a social fact.
Explanations for differences in the rates of suicide in two different
societies or social groups (numbering in millions) cannot be sought
at the individual level—we must look to social factors that affect the
group as a whole. This is why the commonsense approach that seeks
to turn data on the under-representation of the lowest castes in the
privileged sections of society into evidence of the 'lack of merit' of
these castes is sociological nonsense. Any individual member of any
caste may do well or not depending on his or her abilities and resources,
but when we speak of *rates* of representation for whole communities
with millions of members, all such inter-individual differences are
averaged out. If genetic explanations are ruled out—as they have been
for a long time—the only reasonable explanation is in terms of the
social mechanisms (whether intentionally or accidentally created) of
systematic discrimination.

In short, significant differences between social groups are not just
another subject for sociological investigation, they are subjects where
such investigation is *privileged*. Why, then, has this subject received so
little attention in Indian sociology? Indeed, with some exceptions, it
would be fair to say that the evidence discussed in this chapter has
been produced without any inputs from Indian sociology. To explain
this situation, it is necessary to consider not only the commonsense
on caste mentioned in the previous section, but also factors specific to
the location of Indian sociology as a discipline, and the location of
caste within this disciplinary space.

Two aspects of the disciplinary positioning of Indian sociology that were discussed in the Introduction are also relevant here—namely, the dominance of economics and the tilt towards anthropology and its methods, both of which have dissuaded macro-analyses of caste inequality. However, we also need to consider other factors that may have discouraged attention from caste inequality, factors that are more specifically related to this particular institution than to the discipline as a whole.

CASTE AS A COLONIAL CONSTRUCT

An influential strand of recent scholarship has argued that the institution of caste as we know it today is largely a modern and specifically colonial invention. In this view, the policies of the colonial state, particularly things like the Census and other attempts to count, codify or document caste, had the effect of 'substantializing' or solidifying what used to be a diffuse and localized institution. The colonial power 'essentialised' caste—thought of it as an essence that defined Indians and Indian culture—and it set out to measure and document this essence. These efforts at measurement brought into existence precisely that which was sought to be measured. From being a fluid, context-dependent variable, caste turned into a fixed, immutable essence. The nexus between colonial power and colonialist forms of knowledge (like anthropology) thus constructed the very version of caste that colonialism needed to cement its own world view.

It is clear that the considerable work done on this aspect of caste has established the basic point it set out to make, namely that state structures and processes influenced the construction and life of 'ascriptive' attributes like caste. However, it is unclear what the relevance of all this is in the context of discussing contemporary caste inequality. At best, the substantialization argument relates to the past origins of caste differences in the modern era; it says little about the current dynamics of this problem. As the evidence discussed in the previous section shows, whether or not it was a historical invention, caste inequality is a matter of contemporary fact. And the institution itself has thrived in post-independence India despite its absence from the Census and its Constitutional abolition. In fact, the caste groups that have had the biggest impact on contemporary politics—the OBCs—are precisely the ones that have never been counted or documented in the last fifty years.

Moreover, we have to remember that the substantialization arguments were intended as counters to the colonialist assertion that Indian culture was defined by caste, that it was its essence. Against such positions, the substantialization scholars (from Bernard Cohn through Arjun Appadurai and Sudipta Kaviraj to Richard Smith, Rashmi Pant and others) have done well to establish the processes of construction and deployment that the category of caste went through. However, knowing that a category is constructed rather than primordial does not help us a great deal in evaluating its social effectivity or gauging its content. (After all, knowing that democracy is a notion borrowed from the West does not really help us to understand contemporary politics in India.) In any case, it is up to those who believe that the colonial origin of caste is relevant to our attempts to deal with it in the present to demonstrate how and why this is so.

Broadly speaking, therefore, the colonial origins thesis has the effect of strengthening commonsense arguments that contemporary caste divisions are basically an imperial legacy from the times when the institution was given a new lease of life by attempts to measure and document it.

ACKNOWLEDGING THE MODERNITY OF CASTE

Perhaps the most important and least understood set of reasons for the relative neglect of caste inequality have to do with the 'bad odour' that has surrounded this category in modern times. In the classic orientalist approach, caste was held out as incontrovertible proof of India's otherness and its failure to meet the standards of modern-Western morality. This was hammered home so hard that it entered the Indian psyche as well, and the beginnings of nationalism could only be made in the reformist mode, by insisting that Indians could be cured of caste, that it did not define the totality of Indian tradition, and so on.

What happened here was that without realizing it we acquiesced in the orientalist characterization of caste as other-than-modern. And because nationalism could not be jump-started without re-claiming modernity, caste got locked into the tradition-modernity axis as an atavism, as a social evil that had been an undeniable and unfortunate part of our past, *where it should stay*. Caste had no place in modern India, as our nationalist leaders never tired of declaring. As soon as we get rid of the colonial conditions and apparatuses which foster and encourage it, it will soon wither away. We were so committed to this prognosis that we believed it to be fact. And anyone who did not sportingly agree to ignore the processes by which it was being systematically reproduced in the modern era was made to pay a price, as the careers of Ambedkar and Lohia illustrate.

Given that most sociologists (like other academics) were from upper-caste backgrounds, they could not call upon the accidental resources of personal experience to overcome the powerful consensual positioning of caste in the past. Thus, Indian sociology was unable to address adequately the forms in which caste was being *reinvented as a modern institution,* specially its new modes of reproduction and the fresh meanings and functions it was acquiring in urban India. Although sociologists were tirelessly documenting the continued existence of the phenomenon, they were doing so from within a disciplinary perspective that placed it primarily in the world of 'tradition', which, in practical terms, meant the village, ritual practices, kinship norms and so on. They were ill-equipped, therefore, to track its progress in modern contexts like big-city Chinese restaurants and among safari-suited, English-speaking people who would be genuinely aghast at the idea that caste was part of their social identity.

CHAPTER SIX

The Centrality of the Middle Class

Class seems to be the social science concept that has suffered the sharpest decline in popularity and prestige during the last decade. This is in strong contrast to the 1970s and '80s , when it had inspired and energized the social sciences in India, particularly history and economics. Since then, the collapse of socialism and the broader disarray of Marxism as a political philosophy and a social scientific perspective have made the riches-to-rags story of class seem so self-evident that it tends to be taken for granted. The current intellectual climate does not encourage a critical examination of the reasons for the marginalization of the class concept.

These reasons may be divided into two broad groups: the first relates to the rise of other concepts and categories that have taken over much of the explanatory ground that class used to occupy, while the second (and older) group concerns the internal inadequacies of class itself. Recent developments—like the rise to prominence of categories like gender, race, and ethnicity; the salience of 'new social movements' organized around non-traditional issues like the environment or peace; and the spread of various types of 'identity politics'—seem to bear little or no direct relation to the changing fortunes of the concept of class. But all of these have certainly deepened the crisis of the class concept and amplified the long-standing complaints about its inadequacies.

As is well known, despite its centrality to his theoretical framework, class is one concept that Marx himself did not develop adequately. Indeed, the explicit theoretical discussion of class in *Capital* is confined to the famous one-and-a-half-page fragment at the end of the unfinished third volume.[1] Thus, what we inherit from the Marxist corpus is an almost entirely *historical* rather than a theoretical discussion of class, as in the classic passages of the *Communist Manifesto*, and the famous essays on French political history, 'The Eighteenth Brumaire of Louis Napoleon' and 'The Class Struggles in France'. Despite their brilliance, the brief examples of class analysis that Marx offers us cannot ensure that his concept is able to bear the enormous *theoretical* burden placed on it.

Theoretically, the concept of class is located at the confluence of economy, society and polity. This is an absolutely vital location given that Marxism's claims to distinctiveness rest precisely on its insistence that the three spheres are interpenetrating and hierarchically-ordered aspects of a single, seamless social world. Thus, 'class' in Marxism is the theoretical principle by which society may be divided into distinct groups that: (a) are identified by their economic role or position, which (b) shapes the social world they inhabit and the culture they fashion, which, in turn, (c) moulds their political consciousness and inspires their actions. It is in this sense that the three spheres are seen as interpenetrating and even integrated with one another. But though integrated, they are also of unequal importance—causal priority is accorded to the economy, or level (a), which is privileged over the other two levels of society/culture (b) and politics (c), with not much of a distinction being made among the latter two. In short, the concept of class is the centrepiece of the core causal sequence proposed by Marxist theory wherein what you *are* (at the economic level) shapes what you *experience* (at the social level) which ultimately determines what you *do* (at the political level).

The power and appeal of the schema are apparent even in such a short and simplified account. History is no longer the will of the gods, the deeds of kings and queens, or the genius of great men and women—

nor is it simply meaningless; rather, its coherence is to be sought in the patterned material realities of everyday life. And though history is a moving, changing, open-ended process, it is also bound by the material circumstances of past and present. What you are sets limits on what you can do, but you still have the relative autonomy to act today in ways that could change what you are tomorrow.

However, by the same token, it is also clear that far too much is being asked of a single concept. Imagine three separate mapping exercises: one to trace the boundaries of groups with distinct economic profiles; the second to identify groups with different socio-cultural ways of life; and the third to define groups with different political interests and agendas. Strictly speaking, the Marxist concept of class is supposed to ensure that the boundaries of these three types of groups coincide exactly when superimposed on each other—that each economic class also has a distinct culture and a specific politics. If this seems an excessively restrictive condition, its origins have to be sought in the fact that, at the theoretical level, Marx conceived of an essentially bipolar world with only two opposed classes, capitalists and workers.[2]

As social scientists have discovered in the century and a half since Marx, the two-class scheme is a very useful heuristic device, particularly for model building in economic and political theory. But its limitations as a tool for empirical social analysis—visible even in Marx's own time—have never been more obvious. The most serious of these limitations is the inability to accommodate classes and groupings other than the two core classes of capital and labour. To the degree that such classes are socially and politically important, we need to go beyond the inherited Marxist corpus for meaningful class analysis.

The 'intermediate' or middle classes have arguably been the most important non-polar classes. Although this is generally true of both Western and non-Western countries at least since the late nineteenth century, there are several reasons why the middle classes have been particularly important in ex-colonial nations. However, this class segment has received relatively little scholarly attention in either context.

In the Indian context in particular, the mismatch between the contemporary importance of the middle class and the volume of reliable research on it is one of the more remarkable anomalies in our social science literature. After D.P. Mukerjee's pioneering reflections (Mukerjee 1948) comes B.B. Misra's classic survey (Misra 1961). No study of comparable breadth and authority has emerged since. Most of the recent work is either not of a scholarly nature, or it is restricted to the colonial period and to specific regions, or more often cities such as Calcutta.[3] This anomaly is partly explained by the fact that the middle class has been a traditional blind spot for both Marxist-left wing and liberal-mainstream social theory. The former has treated it as an acute theoretical 'embarrassment' (Wright 1985:13) or a 'swamp' of ambiguity (Lefebvre 1976:25), while the latter has tended to 'naturalize' it by uncritically adopting its world view.[4] A peculiarly Indian factor may also have been at work: the middle class may have seemed an 'unworthy' or self-indulgent topic for a generation of social scientists drawn from this class, who believed that their mandate was to act on behalf of 'the people' who constituted the nation.

The Social Significance of the Middle Class

As is well known, the founders of Marxism had little regard for the middle classes, or the 'petit bourgeoisie' in their terminology. Unlike the bourgeoisie and, of course, the proletariat, which were considered to be great classes with a historic mission, the intermediate classes were seen as impediments to the progressive march of history. This is despite the explicit acknowledgement in the *Communist Manifesto*, no less, that the leaders of the proletarian revolution would be recruited from its ranks. We have to wait until the advent of Antonio Gramsci for a more careful and constructive Marxist analysis of the middle classes and their role in modern capitalist societies. It is mainly to Gramsci that we are indebted for seminal insights into the general importance of the middle classes in creating and maintaining the dominant ideology that regulates the social structure.

This is also the preliminary reason for the significance of the middle classes: their disproportionate influence in ideological matters. The most immediate evidence of this is to be found in the attractiveness of this class as a social location. Although it is true that the middle class is a notoriously loose term, it is striking that hardly anyone wishes to decline membership and even those who are ineligible wish to be included in it. Why is the middle class viewed as such a desirable social location? The answer has to be sought in the many meanings attached to the 'middleness' of this class.

In popular commonsense—much of which is produced by/in the middle class itself—the middle class is projected as an 'average' class that best represents the whole of society. It may be useful to borrow some terms from statistics to understand the different strands of meaning involved in this notion of the average.

Descriptive statistics is all about 'data reduction'—reducing unmanageable amounts of information to manageable proportions—and it depends heavily on averages, because an average is a single number that can 'stand for' or represent any group of numbers, however large. The three most common averages in statistics are the mean, the median and the mode. The mean (or arithmetic mean) of a set of numbers is the sum total of their values divided by the number of members in the set; because of its mathematical properties, the mean is considered the most 'powerful' average and is by far the most heavily used. If all the numbers in a set are arranged in ascending or descending order, the median represents the midpoint of the set; its main advantage is that (unlike the mean) it is a very stable average that is not distorted by the presence of extreme values. The mode represents the value that occurs most frequently in a set of numbers; unlike the mean and median which are artificial constructs, the mode generally refers to an actually existing value in the set, the one that is most common.

Working by analogy, we can unravel the various strands of meaning that are woven into the notion of middleness associated with the middle class. The most obvious is the 'neither-nor' notion of avoiding extremes associated with the median: the middle class is thought of (and more importantly, thinks of itself) as the stable centre of society and polity impervious to extremes. Thus the middle class is supposed to be neither poor nor rich, neither too conservative nor progressive, and so on, in a familiar litany that sees virtue in moderation and claims to embody it. Somewhere along the way, through mechanisms that we still don't know enough about, this straightforward, median-like notion of middleness also acquires (or claims) the mode-like quality of representing the most frequent or popular values in society.

Deferring a more detailed discussion, let me offer a quick illustration: 'the common man' is a familiar phrase used in the media and everyday discourse; it is also the name given to the iconic figure created by veteran cartoonist R.K. Laxman. By a remarkable feat of ideological condensation, this phrase/figure manages to convey a powerful sense of middle-class identity that claims to be 'common' both in the sense of something that is *shared* as well as something that is *widespread*. Further along on its semantic journey, the notion of middleness is inflated into a larger sense of *legitimate representativeness*— the middle class is projected as the social group that is the best qualified to represent the whole of society (or be the most 'rigorous' average in the sense of the arithmetic mean). Thus, the reasons why 'everyone' would like to belong to the middle class have to do with the various kinds of desirability that are attached to its middleness, ranging from the position of a 'centrist' group avoiding extremes, through the general sense of representing the majority, to a full-blown assertion of moral legitimacy as the group most qualified to act or speak on behalf of society.

The initial justification for the social significance of the middle class is therefore directly linked to the claim that it is 'the class that is everywhere represented as representing everyone' (Ehrenreich 1989:3). But this is a claim that needs to be evaluated, and here we encounter the familiar problem of the 'derivative' or at least the late comer status of non-Western and specially colonial nations. The specific senses of middleness discussed above have obviously been influenced by the history of the emergence and subsequent development of the middle classes in Western nations, and this sometimes makes for anomalies in non-Western contexts.

The most striking example of this concerns the 'modal' claim of middleness, namely the claim that the middle classes represent the major (or most numerous) section of society. This claim has been a more or less legitimate one in most Western countries, at least since around the middle of the twentieth century. The bout of unprecedented prosperity that followed World War II meant that the middle classes (broadly defined) began to account for the largest plurality if not an actual majority of the population. Only a small proportion could be classified as upper class, and the ranks of the poor and even the traditional working class were thinned out by a combination of rising incomes and economic restructuring which relocated jobs in the tertiary or service sector. There is thus some justification—at least in purely numerical terms—for the representative claims of the Western middle classes, if defined broadly as 'middle income' groups. Matters are starkly different in poor countries like India, and it is necessary to enter into questions of definition in order to understand these differences.

DEFINING THE MIDDLE CLASS

How we define the middle (or any other) class depends on what we wish to do with the concept. Take, for example, the three components of the Marxist definition of class discussed earlier—the economic, the social and the political. The economic definition aims to identify groups with shared economic characteristics, such as levels or sources of income, ownership of particular kinds of wealth or property, place in the economic structure, and so on. The social definition attempts to demarcate groups that share the same lifestyles, patterns of consumption, or social attitudes. The political definition tries to differentiate groups according to the political agendas or parties they support, or the leaders they identify with. Underlying such theoretical definitions is a larger analytical strategy or logic, some set of reasons why being able to identify groups of a given type would help us understand society better. At this theoretical level, definitions are judged by their logical clarity and rigour, and, ultimately, by the insights they promise.

However, once we move to the level of empirical social analysis, this is not enough—we also have to worry about translating our definitions into concrete, observable criteria. Compromises are inevitable here, for there is always a gap between what we can conceptualize in theory and what we can see and measure in the real world. Even the simplest of theoretical definitions runs into complications at the empirical level. Take, for instance, the most straightforward economic definition of class based on levels of income and wealth. If there were a list of all citizens that also told us about their income levels, we could 'classify' each person, determine the size of each class at the national or regional levels, and so on. Of course, there is no such list, so we have to begin improvising.

Shall we use data from the Central Board of Direct Taxes that tells us how many taxpayers there are, and their division by levels of income? But this tells us only about a tiny minority of the population that pays taxes—it leaves out the vast majority whose incomes are below the taxable limit; all those dependent on agricultural incomes (which are not taxed); and all those who are either legally avoiding or illegally evading taxes. We could use the consumption expenditure data collected by the National Sample Survey Organization (some of which was discussed in the last chapter). But if we do so, we are moving away from the theoretical basis for our definition, namely income. Consumption expenditure may be a good proxy for income, but it *is* a proxy, and it involves compromises. For example, relying on consumption expenditure data tends to seriously underestimate the income of the rich and to (relatively) overstate that of the poor, because a smaller proportion of income is spent on consumption as we go up the income scale. (The rich get rich by accumulating income and wealth faster than they can spend it, whereas the poor may often be spending their income faster than they can earn it, that is, they may be living on credit.) All the difficulties discussed so far are *conceptual* and would apply even when the data collection process is assumed to be perfect. This is never true, of course, and we must also consider the problems of errors, omissions and biases specific to particular data sources (for example, in the case of the NSSO data, its under-representation of urban non-poor households, or its sensitivity to the reference period). Thus, empirical considerations may lead us away from the conceptual attributes decided upon in theory.

The main point of this extended example is to illustrate the logic of definitions. All definitions are motivated by a larger theoretical purpose and are more or less arbitrary—they prompt us to use one set of criteria (rather than other possible ones) in the hope that this will yield useful insights. However, theoretical definitions can never be operationalized in their exact form because the available empirical indicators never match the definitional criteria perfectly—there is always some 'slippage' or gap between the two. It is not the existence of this gap, but its extent that is important in judging the worth of a definition. As long as it is empirically plausible, a good definition is one that is 'good to think with'.

Thus, contrary to what commonsense might suggest, defining a class is less about correctly identifying a pre-existing social group, and more about deciding what kind of social group it is useful to identify. Of course, 'useful' here means helpful for understanding society, so it is clear that only information on really existing groups is relevant. But the opposite is not true—just because a group exists, it does not follow that knowing about it will help us analyse or understand society better.

This distinction has often got obscured in discussions about the Indian middle class in the media and in popular literature. For these and other reasons, the conceptual rationale for particular definitions of the middle class, and the various kinds of slippage involved in its empirical identification have not received the careful attention they demand.

THE MIDDLE CLASS AS 'CONSUMER CLASS'

The simplest definitions of the middle class have been those that have conceived of it in purely economic terms as a specific segment of consumers. During the early 1990s, when the new economic policy of liberalization was getting underway, there was considerable excitement among marketing experts about the huge numbers of potential consumers that this class might offer to global corporations entering the Indian market for the first time since Independence. Some went so far as to estimate the size of this 'consuming class' at around 300 million, or 30 per cent of the Indian population. A decade later, it is clear that these overblown estimates were the products of the deliberate hype stoked by vested interests.

Even if it is easy to conclude that 30 per cent is far too high a number, we still have to determine where to draw the lines that distinguish the middle class from other classes. It seems obvious that the middle class should exclude the rich and the poor, however we define these categories; but it is not so clear whether the middle class should include everyone who is non-rich and non-poor. Is the middle class a purely negative and residual category, or should it also involve some positive characteristics? At this point, it becomes impossible to avoid discussing absolute levels of income.

Table 1 (based on data from the NSSO's 55th Round survey) provides a summary statement of the distribution of the monthly per capita consumption expenditure in India during 1999-2000. Where on this spectrum would we locate 'the middle class', and for what reasons?

This stark and simple question helps us to pinpoint the sources of confusion in even the simplest 'consumer-segment' definition of the middle class. Let us note, to begin with, that defining the middle class as merely a grouping of consumers does not involve any explicit stipulation of the *levels* or *types* of consumption. Nevertheless, it is clear that the 'Below the Poverty Line' category is not in contention for inclusion in the middle class because this category will not be participating in formal markets in any significant way. All the consumption of people in this category will be routed through informal markets tied to employers and/or creditors of various types. But everyone from the 'Above the Poverty Line' category upwards is presumably participating in formal markets to a significant degree: who do we include and who do we exclude from the middle class?

TABLE 1
Estimated Class Composition of the Indian Population
Based on Monthly Percapita Consumption Expenditure Data, NSSO, 1999-2000

	Rural India		Urban India	
Description of Class	Monthly Per Capita Expenditure Class	Per cent of Popn	Per cent of Popn	Monthly Per Capita Expenditure Class
Below Poverty Line Population	Rs 329 or Less	34.4	29.6	Rs 458 or Less
Above Poverty Line Next 4 classes	Rs 329 to Rs 470	33.8	36.9	Rs 458 to Rs 775
Less Poor Next 4 classes	Rs 470 to Rs 775	24.7	25.9	Rs 775 to Rs 1,500
Non Poor Top 2 classes	Rs 775 or More	7.0	7.6	Rs 1,500 or more
	All Classes	100	100	All Classes

Note: Rs 329 & Rs 458 were the official (Planning Commission) estimates of the Poverty Line for Rural and Urban India, respectively, in 1999-2000. Source: NSSO 55th Round

It is amply evident at this stage that to speak of 'the middle class' as a single entity is not very helpful. The obvious solution (adopted by most market surveys) is to divide the spectrum of consumers into different levels or segments such as 'A', 'B', 'C'; or 'upper-', 'middle-' and 'lower-middle class', and so on. Note, however, that it makes sense to continue to refer to these segments as belonging to a larger class called 'the middle class' only if they have more in common with each other than they have with groups outside the middle class. This is a matter for empirical investigation in each given context, but is often forgotten or deliberately ignored. For example, a group that is actually part of the upper class (in terms of lifestyle, income levels, attitudes or other criteria) may prefer to conceal or play down this fact by insisting on calling itself the 'upper-middle class'. On the other hand, a group that is actually part of the lower class may wish to pass itself off as 'lower-middle class', and so on.

In short, the everyday term 'middle class' is more of a symbolic than a factual description. It is chosen or avoided for its social connotations rather than its accuracy, just as the 'right address' indicates social status rather than mere geographical location. Sociologists and others who wish to understand the world around them must be alert to this aspect of the 'middle class', specially in contexts where inordinate attention is being paid to questions of size. Even when a straightforward classification of consumers is being attempted, we must go beyond seemingly self-explanatory terms like 'middle class' to make explicit the underlying assumptions about levels and types of consumption.

In practical terms, this means that we must confront all claims about the size or the growth of the middle class with the sort of data that is presented in Table 1. To put the matter provocatively, all claims about the size of the Indian middle class must be faced with the absolute levels of consumption expenditure that are implied by the claim. For example, let us suppose that I claim that the urban middle class includes the top 33 per cent of the population of urban India. Translating this claim into the figures available in Table 1, this includes the top two categories in urban India (which together account for a little over 33 per cent of the urban population). This means that my definition of the urban middle class includes everyone with a monthly per capita consumption expenditure of Rs 775 or more, or families of five spending Rs 3,875 per month or more. This gives us a rough but very concrete picture of the sort of people who would have to be included in this definition of the middle class. We can then check whether the definition is plausible and consistent.

One complaint that has often been made about NSSO data in particular is that it seems to underestimate levels of consumption, specially among the non-poor. Past research suggests that there may be some truth to this, and so it is important to turn to other sources of nationwide data to see if this makes a difference to notions of the middle class.

Table 2 presents data on possession of consumer durables from the Market Information Survey of Households (MISH), a huge annual nationwide survey conducted by the National Council for Applied Economic Research. MISH has a sample size of 3,00,000 households which is much larger than the 1,20,000 for the NSSO big sample surveys. Moreover, 70 per cent of the MISH sample is devoted to urban India because the survey is interested in consumption of manufactured goods. However, because of its large sample size, the absolute sample for rural areas in MISH is larger than the absolute size of the NSSO rural sample. It can thus be argued that MISH is a useful counterpoint to the NSSO survey reported in Table 1.[5]

TABLE 2
Possession of Consumer Durables by Indian Households
Percentage of households that own the relevant consumer durable item

Consumer Durable Item	Rural India		Urban India		All India	
	1985-86	1995-96	1985-86	1995-96	1985-86	1995-96
Bicycle	30.3	52.9	35.2	48.6	31.7	51.7
Scooter	0.6	2.1	6.1	15.9	2.1	6.0
Motorcycle	0.7	1.9	2.6	5.6	1.2	2.9
Pressure Cooker	3.4	13.0	32.5	56.3	11.3	25.3
Mixer/Grinder	0.6	3.1	10.9	30.1	3.4	10.8
Refrigerator	0.3	2.0	8.8	25.2	2.6	8.6
B&W TV Set	1.0	15.4	15.1	45.6	4.7	24.0
Colour TV Set	0.1	2.6	4.0	21.2	1.2	7.9
Washing Machine	0.0	0.5	1.4	10.9	0.4	3.5

All figures in percentages, rounded to nearest decimal. Source: I. Natarajan (ed.), *India Market Demographics Report 1998*, National Council for Applied Economic Research, Chapter 4.

Since the possession of consumer durables is a common indicator of class status, Table 2 provides a useful overview of the probable size of the middle class defined in different ways.

Table 2 also reiterates the sobering message of Table 1: there is little room for extravagant estimates of the size of the middle class when less than 8 per cent of Indian households possessed a colour TV set in 1995-96; less than 9 per cent possessed a refrigerator; and only 6 per cent owned a scooter. Even a pressure cooker was owned by only about 25 per cent of households.

Such confrontation with concrete data alerts us to the possible biases that may be involved in statements made about the middle class. It also helps establish two general features of the Indian middle class considered as a class of consumers, even when levels of consumption are not specified: on the one hand, in terms of absolute numbers, this may be a very large class by world standards; on the other hand, it is a very small proportion of the Indian population, although its magnitude can vary somewhat according to the precise definition chosen. This is why the claim that the middle class represents 'everyone'—though it is usually implied rather than explicitly stated—is so clearly untenable in India.

Empirical exercises like this allow us to detect the ideological sleights of hand by which the middle class presents itself as a large plurality representing everyone, although it is, in fact, a small minority that usually speaks only for itself. When confronted with such claims to representation, it is always useful to examine the concrete social or economic location of the groups being spoken for or doing the speaking. The next time you see an R.K. Laxman cartoon or watch a post-budget television show, remind yourself that 'the common man' belongs to the top 10 or 15 per cent of the income distribution. This may make you feel slightly odd, which is a welcome sign that you are looking beyond commonsense.

But one has to remind oneself at the same time that the size of a class is certainly not the only or the most important indication of its social significance. It is only because of the mismatch between the claimed and actual strength of the middle class that questions of its size are relevant. This does not mean, of course, that 'big' classes are good, that minorities are always insignificant, or that numerical strength is always relevant. The more important point about the 'consumer-segment' definition of the middle class is that it is much too narrow to capture the critical, multidimensional, role of the middle class in post-colonial societies.

ALTERNATIVE THEORETICAL DEFINITIONS OF THE MIDDLE CLASS

Here are three hypothetical definitions of the middle class that may be 'good to think with'. They are theoretical definitions, and are prompted mainly by their promise in highlighting crucial aspects of post-colonial societies. However, their empirical plausibility must also be examined, and possible sources of empirical evidence explored.

1. The middle class is the class that *articulates* the hegemony of the ruling bloc; it both (a) *expresses* this hegemony by translating the relations of domination into the language of legitimization; and (b) *mediates* the relationship between classes within the ruling bloc, as well as between this bloc and other classes.

The term articulation is being used here in the double sense of giving voice to, as well as linking or connecting in a flexible manner.[6] As a member of the ruling bloc, the middle class is responsible for managing the discourse of legitimization; this includes both the process of production of this discourse, as well as the subsidiary practices necessary to ensure that it 'takes hold' as the common sense of everyday life. Secondly, this class helps to manage the relations between industrial-financial and agrarian capital within the ruling bloc, and to mediate the relations between the ruling bloc and the rest of society. The importance of the middle class is greatly enhanced by the fact that coalition is the necessary form of the ruling bloc—in post-colonial India, no single class is in a position to build hegemony alone (Kaviraj 1988).

The main axis around which hegemony is built—and which also explains the peculiar centrality of the middle class—is the developmental state. In the early years of independence, the transfer of legitimacy, power and moral prestige from the middle-class leaders of the freedom movement to the masters of the newly autonomous state was almost seamless. As is well known, conditions of colonial backwardness produced a remarkably inclusive consensus on the need for state-led, industry-based investment programmes on a massive scale. The hegemony of the ruling bloc thus had to operate through, and in the shadow of, the developmental state, which, in turn, was critically dependent on middle class administrative and technical functionaries.

Given that, during the Nehruvian era, the dominant legitimizing ideology (development) speaks in the idiom of 'patriotic production' (Deshpande 1993), the middle class (and the state apparatus that it controls) adopts the posture of the 'proxy'—of *representing* (acting on behalf of) the true protagonists of national history, the patriotic producers. The technicization of development, and the enormous prestige of scientific technology also provide the middle class with a significant measure of legitimacy.

2. The middle class is the class that is most dependent on *cultural capital* and on the mechanisms for the reproduction of such capital.

Cultural capital is undoubtedly a form of property that remains under-researched both theoretically and specially empirically. Even the few available attempts to theorize it (such as those of Alvin Gouldner or Pierre Bourdieu) need to be adapted and modified before they can speak to the Indian situation.[7] But there can be little doubt that the middle class more than any other is defined by its ownership and control of cultural capital.

For the middle class, such cultural capital may consist of particular types of *identities* (caste, community, or region) and *competences* (educational credentials, linguistic and other social skills).[8] Such forms of cultural capital fulfil at least three attributes of property: they confer tangible and psychological benefits; they can be privatized, that is, others can be excluded from enjoying their benefits; and, finally, they can be transmitted across generations. However, the mode of its reproduction, transmission or inheritance is unique: an identity or skill cannot simply be handed over from person to person (as other economic assets can), but has to be learnt afresh. At the same time, this does not mean that everyone has equal access to cultural capital—as with other forms of capital, initial endowments play a decisive role. Cultural capital is also peculiar in that it includes characteristic patterns of *consumption*, as Bourdieu (1984) has shown. Such consumption is to be conceived in a broad sense, to include not only the consumption of commodities and services but also of more abstract cultural entities such as ideologies, beliefs and stereotypes.

But the most complicating aspect of cultural capital is that it is frequently invisible as *property*, but is socially misrecognized as innate ability, or 'merit'. Members of the middle-class are, as a rule, owners of cultural capital; they may also possess innate talents, be hardworking, disciplined and so on. But in the self-image of the class, its achievements are solely due to innate ability, never to inherited cultural capital. The important question is whether cultural capital can be treated on a par with other forms of capital (e.g. land, wealth, and so on) and be *subjected to social regulation* in the same way. Is it to be treated as an 'ascriptive' or an 'achieved' attribute? To what extent can society tolerate, encourage or redress disparities in this form of capital? These are critical issues not only for the middle class, but also for the rest of society.

3. As an increasingly *differentiated* class, the middle class specializes in the production and dissemination of ideologies; its elite fraction specializes in the *production* of ideologies, and its mass fraction engages in the exemplary *consumption* of these ideologies, thus investing them with social legitimacy.

In concrete terms, the elite segment of the middle class can be thought of as including the 'intelligentsia' in the usual sense (Béteille 1989), with a special emphasis on professional politicians, top bureaucrats, media persons, intellectuals and other 'specialists in legitimization' as Gramsci puts it. The primary function of this segment is to produce and transmit legitimizing ideologies along with the peripheral social practices necessary to sustain them. However, such an elite fraction by itself does not have the necessary social weight—the moral volume and density that Durkheim spoke of—to make these ideologies take root in the everyday life of the community. The 'mass' segment of the middle class performs the vital function of lending weight and apparent substance to these ideologies through force of example. By playing out their role as committed and sincere believers of the dominant ideologies, the mass section of the middle class (what are commonly referred to as the middle-middle as well as the lower-middle classes) enables such ideologies to take root, to 'stick'.[9]

Although the above definitions are hypothetical ones suggested as food for thought, some indication of the ways in which they might be useful for understanding the Indian middle class can be found in the following historical account.

Middleness in the social history of the Indian middle class(es)

Three main reasons have been offered for the special salience of the middle classes in colonial contexts: (1) in peripheral societies characterized by 'backward' capitalism mediated by colonial rule, the industrial bourgeoisie is a relatively weak class, and the intermediate classes (specially the intelligentsia and the professional-technical-managerial elite) is correspondingly much stronger than in Western contexts; (2) in such societies, the major thrust towards capitalist development occurs after independence under the aegis of the developmental state, and the middle classes dominate the state apparatus; (3) partly because of the above two reasons and partly because they often play a leading role in anti-colonial struggles, the intermediate or middle classes enjoy great political legitimacy which prompts them to go beyond their 'intermediate' status and try to reproduce themselves as a dominant class (Ahmad 1996).

In India (as in many ex-colonies), the contemporary importance of the middle class and its post-colonial trajectory were shaped by its colonial role. Indeed, Indian nationalism was initially a creation of this class. The imperial power was compelled by circumstance to allow this class to educate and Westernize itself so that it could supply the subaltern bureaucracy needed to administer the vast colony. At the same time, it could not be allowed the full measure of its ambitions, which were inevitably thwarted at some point. It is these disgruntled elites who helped give birth to the idea of the nation, and in time, to a nationalist movement (Anderson 1991). As is well known, middle-class professionals (specially lawyers) dominated the middle and upper level leadership of the Indian National Congress (Misra 1961).

It is hardly surprising, therefore, that this class acquired a stranglehold on the state apparatus after independence, and was elevated to the position of an indispensable member of the ruling bloc, the dominant segments of which were agrarian capitalists and the industrial and financial bourgeoisie (Kaviraj 1988, Rudra 1989, Bardhan 1989, Beteille 1989, Iyer 1989). Given that this class helped to create and maintain a 'native' public sphere in the colony (Chatterjee 1994), it carried over this role into the post-colonial period.

Perhaps the main function of the middle class was to *build hegemony*.[10] This was a function it partly inherited from the Western history of modernization/capitalist development and the emergence there of the contemporary forms of the bourgeois-democratic nation-state with a rapidly evolving economy. By the late nineteenth century, the Western role model of the middle class, (as famously articulated by ideologues like Matthew Arnold) was ready for export and adaptation. The members of the emergent Indian middle class—urban professionals, white-collar workers in government and industry, and the intelligentsia—self-consciously invoked this model based on a *moral privileging* of the middle class.[11]

In the Indian context, this moral privileging took the form, during the colonial period, of an ethical imperative to launch and manage the nationalist revival in the now familiar strategy: modernizing by imitating the West in the 'outer/material' sphere, while at the same time reinventing a classicized tradition protected from Western contamination in the 'inner/spiritual' sphere (Chatterjee 1986). The post-independence form of this moral privileging took the form of 'development'—the middle class saw itself as continuing the nationalist project by managing the developmental process on behalf of the nation.

THE MIDDLE CLASS AND THE IDEOLOGY AND PROCESSES OF DEVELOPMENT

Although we refer to them as members of the middle classes, the leaders of the nationalist movement were mostly members of the social elite who had taken to the new urban professions, particularly the law. It is only in the post-independence phase of Indian history that the middle classes in the contemporary sense emerged, consisting of people who were not substantial property owners, and who were dependent on educational and cultural capital and the professional careers that these promised.

This post-independence middle class was entirely a product of the developmental regime. This was true both at the ideological and institutional levels. Ideologically, the particular notion of development that held sway in the Nehruvian era conceived of it as primarily a scientific-technical process over which professional experts should preside. The state, assisted by such experts, would bring about development on behalf of and for the people who needed and wanted it. In retrospect, this was a very de-politicized and top-down version of development that saw no active role for the people themselves, who were projected as lacking the technical expertise required to plan and execute development projects. But such a model of development gave pride of place to the middle classes who formed the professional and technical workforce. Institutionally as well, the state-led model of development gave primacy to the bureaucracy, once again a preserve of the middle classes.

If this was the 'demand' side of the mutually supportive

relationship between the middle class and the developmental state, there was also the 'supply' side. The massive expansion of higher education and the strong emphasis on scientific and technical training swelled the ranks of the middle classes. Most significantly, all this was seen not as providing unprecedented opportunity and encouragement for the middle class, but as part of the great task of nation building. The middle class itself could participate in this task in the same spirit of high-minded dedication that pervaded all state initiatives in these initial years of unbounded hope and optimism.

This Nehruvian high-mindedness and the powerful sense of moral legitimacy that it engendered was an important factor in rendering invisible the unequal benefits that development brought to different classes, castes and regional groups. This could not be kept up indefinitely, however, and eventually the failures and unforeseen consequences of the development process helped undermine the ideology of development. Although they were not noticed at the time, the chain reactions were set in motion in the early post-independence period. These led, by the mid-1960s, to a pervasive multidimensional crisis that ended the Nehru era and decisively changed the trajectory of the nation.

It hardly needs stating today that the development idea is no longer dominant. What needs to be emphasized, however, is that its decline was only partly due to its own failures. In other words, it is not so much that the development process itself has failed—the historical record on this count is a mixed one—but that development-as-ideology no longer resonates with the changed ideological context at the national and global levels. Just as this context once exaggerated the promise of development, today it is magnifying its real and apparent failures. It is not coincidental that the decline of the developmental state is accompanied by the differentiation of the middle class which had experienced a phenomenal growth under its nurturance.

The rhetoric of the Nehruvian era had seemed to issue an inclusive invitation to all members of the nation to come and play the role of the secular-modern citizen devoted to the task of nation building. However, despite the absence of any overt attempt to constitute an exclusive (rather than an inclusive) audience—despite, that is, their apparent 'openness'—nationalist narratives also served to differentiate rather than unite. As it became clear retrospectively, even that most modern and universal of languages, Nehruvian secular-socialism, had harboured subtle strategies of exclusion and selection. The secular modern citizen, though he remained unmarked in public discourse, turned out upon closer examination to be the simultaneously familiar-and-elusive middle-class subject who continues to claim the pre-modern privileges of community, caste, gender and region.

Caste was a particularly prominent marker of this middle-class subject, as discussed in the previous chapter. One indication of this can be found in the fact that, in everyday language, the term 'middle class' often functions as a code word for 'upper caste'. It is only very recently that the stranglehold of the upper castes on all middle-class jobs, specially in the technical-administrative sectors, has been loosened. The NSSO data for 1999-2000 discussed in the previous chapter suggest that the Hindu upper castes are heavily over-represented in the top-most MPCE class in both the rural and specially the urban areas. They account for approximately 59 per cent of this class (Rs 1,925 or more) in urban areas, and around 40 per cent of this class (Rs 950 or more) in the rural areas, although they account for only about 18 per cent of the rural and around 27 per cent of the urban population.[12]

THE DIFFERENTIATION OF THE MIDDLE CLASS

It is not surprising that the possible consequences of the symbiotic relationship between the developmental state and the middle classes were poorly understood in the Nehru era. The standard approach was the naïve, unidimensional one of 'increasing the pool of scientific and technical manpower'. Such an instrumental view failed to accord any agency to this 'pool': that it could constitute a powerful pressure group with desires and ambitions of its own do not seem to have been anticipated. It was only with the emergence of the 'brain drain' phenomenon in the late 1960s and early '70s that the problem drew attention. By this time, however, both as a cause and partly as a consequence of the weakening of the ideology of development, one could no longer be confident that the middle class, the developmental state, and the nation were marching in step.

While the issue awaits detailed investigation, it would seem that the middle class during the Nehru era was not only smaller in absolute size, but also relatively more homogenous than it appears to be today. (Or, perhaps a more accurate way of putting this might be that only a relatively homogenous fraction of the middle class was centrally involved with the Nehruvian enterprise, the regional middle class and other such less homogenous elements being excluded.) There seem to have been two major growth spurts, which also resulted in greater diversification of this class: one during the late 1960s and early '70s , the other in the decade since the mid-1980s. As an initial hypothesis, one might surmise that the first spurt marked the end of Nehruvian 'development', while the second presaged the era of 'globalization'.

The task of identifying the different coherent fractions of the contemporary middle class is an urgent one. Undertaking this conceptual-empirical exercise may, in fact, render the term 'middle class' redundant, which is an unsatisfactory one to begin with. What could be the various axes along which we might differentiate all members of that residual income group (not rich, and not poor) which forms the candidate pool for this class? The answer would depend, of course, on what we wish to do with our definitions/criteria (Wright 1985); what follows is only an illustrative list of possible criteria.

If our aim is to examine the role played by this class in building and maintaining the hegemony of the ruling bloc (as was suggested above), a first cut distinction could be made between the 'elite' and 'mass' fractions of the class, the one mainly involved in producing and the other in consuming legitimizing ideologies. This would produce something like an intelligentsia vs. lower- and middle-middle class split (Rudra 1989).

Another possible axis of differentiation could be the type of cultural capital owned by different fractions of this class. This would produce something like an occupational distribution, with technical-professional groups, generalist administrators, the so-called 'liberal professions', various categories of white-collar workers, and so on.

Access to languages could be an interesting indicator of the social character of different middle-class fractions. One could imagine a division into: monolingual English speakers; a large bi-lingual segment consisting of a) those whose first language is English, but who have a firm link with some Indian language; and b) those whose first language is an Indian one, but who are confident in English as well; and finally, a large group which is rooted in Indian languages and has no real access to English.

A more broad-based division between the globalized, metropolitan, and regional fractions is also possible. This would give due weightage to the sphere of influence/action of each fraction. To these should perhaps be added (at least since the green revolution) a rural-based fraction, which continues to have its main base in the rural/agrarian sector but is also a significant actor in the regional urban centres.

Whatever be the actual ways in which the middle class may have become differentiated, the basic assertion being made here is about the fact of differentiation. The loss of hegemony experienced by the ideology of development is related to this process of differentiation; the ideology loses its addressees, its audience. As various fractions of the middle class evolved in their different ways, their perceived self-interests took them further and further away from the nation-state and the divergence between the ideology of development and the middle class increased over time. In essence, for the most influential and powerful elite fraction of this class (which would have supplied the second generation of Nehruvians), the *nation is no longer the canvas for their dreams and aspirations*. This is due to the decline of old ideologies as much as the rise of new ones—the emergence of sub-national loyalties as well as the lure of transnational identities.

GLOBALIZATION AND THE NEW MIDDLE CLASSES

Ideologies, as Louis Althusser has taught us, are relational phenomena; the tree falling in the forest makes a sound only when there is someone to hear it. It is when a connection is made between a 'message' and its 'addressee'—when a person or social group feels themselves addressed (interpellated, hailed) by an ideology—that it becomes effective. The rise of the new ideologies of 'adjustment' and 'globalization' must therefore be understood partly in terms of the emergence of 'new publics' who see themselves reflected in the identities they offer. The differentiation of the Nehruvian middle class has created new audiences that invest these ideologies with meaning.

Who are the publics addressed by adjustment and globalization? What do they promise to whom? Why do these groups believe in these promises? These questions, once again, await investigation. While there may be a significant body of work now on the sectoral impact of adjustment and globalization—the economic promises it makes to different classes or economic groups—the socio-cultural aspects of these equations are still to be studied. For the point is that the direct or most important *economic* beneficiaries may not necessarily be the most effective or important forces responsible for the success of the ideology.

In a wide-ranging argument on the possibilities presented by globalization, Arjun Appadurai (1997) has suggested that new, 'post-patriotic' identities may be emerging today. The intensified global flows of images, ideas, people, capital and technology have led to a situation where national borders can no longer contain 'diasporic' identities. Such identities may soon offer more progressive and emancipatory alternatives to national identities.

The implications of this argument are such as to pre-empt the whole question of comparisons with development. Appadurai sees great promise in the transcendent ideologies, organizations and identities spawned by globalization. Such a transnational telos could provide a substitute for development, one that does not require the nation-state as its condition of possibility. In fact, the reach of these transnational identities and organizations is such that they can even act as a check on the predatory nation state (for example, Amnesty International, or politically powerful groups of 'non-resident' nationals).[13]

The constituency for such a view is likely to be found among privileged diasporics newly exposed to, and seduced by, the charms of a multicultural existence in a globalized world. However, this is already being recognized as too naïve a view, as shown by the recent controversies around the differences (of class, gender, nationality, ethnicity and so on) which distance different fractions of this cosmopolitan group from each other. Perhaps one needs to concede to it the ambiguity that is claimed on its behalf, but this too is far from being a settled question.

But if there is one class for whom the benefits of globalization seem to clearly outweigh the costs, it is the middle class, particularly its upper (managerial-professional) segment. This class segment is today interpellated by globalization in the same (or perhaps more intense) way that, a generation or two ago, it identified itself with development. Indeed, much of the celebratory rhetoric about globalization emanates from, and is aimed at, this group. Having consolidated its social, economic and political standing on the basis of the developmental state, this group is now ready to kick it away as the ladder it no longer needs.

This class segment has experienced no discontinuity between development and globalization—it has made the transition smoothly. Accompanying this transition is a change in its social stance vis-à-vis other groups within the nation. From its position as a 'proxy' for the nation, this class has now graduated to thinking of itself as a 'portrait' of the nation.[14] That is to say, the middle class no longer claims merely to represent the people (who alone were thought to constitute the nation in the era of development), but rather that it is itself the nation. Evidence of this change in the world view (and self-image) of the middle class elite can be found all around us; its consequences are only just becoming visible.

CHAPTER SEVEN

Globalization and the Geography of Cultural Regions

There is something almost inevitable about globalization being the subject of the last chapter in this book. Almost every previous chapter—whether on modernity, the nation, *hindutva*, or the middle class—has seemed to gravitate towards this theme. And yet, for all its newness, nobody seems to need an introduction to globalization. Among the latest additions to contemporary commonsense, the concept is now ubiquitous not only in the media and popular culture but also in academia. Like other terms that gain sudden currency, globalization asks us to assume that its meaning—and its usefulness—are already self-evident.[1]

In its most general sense, globalization is used as a name for the contemporary era, the present that we inhabit. The point of the term is thus to mark the distinctiveness of this era compared to others in the past. Among the many criteria that claim to capture the specificity of the present two are particularly important, even definitive: *spatiality* and *transnationalism*. Globalization is most commonly understood, indeed it is usually equated with, a new regime of spatiality that is founded on the transnationalization of society. Despite seeming to be strongly self-evident, both strands are more complex than they first appear.

There is something ironic about the equation of globalization with transnationalism, because it privileges precisely the entity that globalization seeks to transcend, namely the nation-state. Thus, in the face of assertions that it is above and beyond national borders, the meaning of globalization remains tied to the notion of the nation-state, which functions as a sort of gate-keeping condition, for it is believed that globalization becomes visible only beyond this threshold. The epochal notion of globalization as a name for our present also begs many questions. It takes but a moment's reflection to realize that transnational connectedness is hardly a distinctive feature of the contemporary era. Colonialism, for instance, was by definition a transnational and global phenomenon; so was classical capitalism, which most world systems theorists believe began in the sixteenth century.

Of course, these initial doubts have their own rejoinders. Proponents of globalization say that it is not the fact of transnationalism but rather its extent and intensity that is important. What is different about the internationalization of social life today is that it affects almost everyone and everything, and it affects them decisively. In short, what is claimed on behalf of globalization as a distinctive era is the *intensification* and *universalization* of transnational flows. These claims certainly seem plausible given the undeniable and substantial increase in global, trans-border flows of images, people, commodities and capital. Considered from the socio-cultural angle, there is surely something unique about the contemporary moment, when cultural resources for the fashioning of identities, media images and all sorts of ethnic groups are criss-crossing the globe, producing startling juxtapositions and unsettling the homogeneity of social spaces.

But what is being claimed on behalf of globalization is actually much more, namely that it has decisively altered the *spatial conditions of possibility* for all kinds of communities, including specially cultural communities. Thus, the materials and mechanisms which shape communities and help sustain them are now 'space neutral', freed of spatial constraints in two senses. First, in the sense that the 'portability' of communities—their movement and transplantation outside the geographical confines of what used to be their 'natural' or historical habitats—is now quite common, such that communities of Sikhs (for example) are now found all over the world and not just in East Punjab. And second, in the sense that the cultural inputs required for many kinds of identity formation are now much more widely dispersed around the globe than they used to be, such that, today, it is possible to become a born-again Christian, a baseball fanatic or a serious student of rock music (for example) almost as easily in Seoul, Chennai, or Lagos as in Sydney, London or Los Angeles.

This, at any rate, is the claim made by the burgeoning literature on the socio-cultural aspects of globalization.[2] However, despite—or perhaps because of—its enthusiasm for the blurring of boundaries, the hybridization of identities or the seamless interfacing of locality and globality, this literature actually tells us very little about the *concrete spatial rearticulations* effected by globalization. An apparatus attuned to change, movement and incongruity cannot help being relatively insensitive to the counterpressure exerted by the resilient but unspectacular continuities present in every specific context. Moreover, the sharp focus on the local and global extremes of the spatial spectrum leaves blurred the intermediate levels of micro-region, region or nation-state. These worries about the concept of globalization form the starting point for this chapter, specially since they seem to be magnified when viewed from a non-Western vantage point like India.

Globalization: Some problems with common usage

There is considerable evidence to support the definition of globalization as a contemporary era in world history marked by major changes in the *spatial logic* governing social institutions and relationships. However, common scholarly and journalistic usage confines the concept to the much more reductive notion of the intensive and extensive *trans-nationalization* of social life. The first problem with the concept is thus its privileging of the very entity it is committed to transcend, namely the nation-state.[3] Not always explicit in theory, this tendency is quite strong in the practice of globalization studies. International phenomena attract attention while others—which may also mark important shifts in spatial logics, but happen not to cross national borders—go unnoticed or are underemphasized. We thus risk missing important changes in the *concrete spatial dynamics* at intermediate levels between the local and the global, such as the national, regional or micro-regional. A corollary risk is that of the artificial inflation of the importance of international effects and phenomena.

To take three examples from the media: the serializing of the *Ramayana* on a newly-expanded national television network was arguably among the most crucial media events that have shaped the cultural-political geography of independent India. While its antecedents or consequences may have had transnational dimensions, this event itself was played out on a national stage. On the other hand, it is well known that the radio programmes of the Sri Lanka Broadcasting Corporation (earlier Radio Ceylon) played a significant role in building a proven national audience for Hindi film music in India during the 1960s and '70s, but the intranational aspects of this phenomenon were perhaps much more important than its international ones. Finally, while the obvious impact of global television software (specially such transnational favourites as *Dallas*, *Santa Barbara*, *Baywatch*, or MTV and its derivatives) is much noticed, this phenomenon may be having an equally important impact on the relations between centres of film-TV production (such as Mumbai, Chennai or Delhi) and their cultural hinterlands, relations which may receive less attention than they deserve because they are inter-regional rather than international.

Apart from the reduction of spatiality to its transnational forms, there are other problems with the way in which the globalization literature identifies its objects of study. Three aspects are particularly noteworthy.

There is an overwhelming emphasis on that which changes or

moves. While this is an understandable bias, awareness of its presence ought to produce countervailing attempts to look at the *apparently unchanging or immobile* aspects of social reality. For it is only when the net effect of change and continuity is known that we can have a true assessment of what has happened and how much of a transformation it represents. It is a truism that most concrete social situations involve *both* change and stability in different degrees, and we need to understand how the two interact rather than confine ourselves to one or the other. (This is true even when the relative weight of the two is greatly unequal.)

Even within the ambit of that which is changing, the globalization literature is disproportionately interested in the incongruous and the exotic. Once again, it is understandable that startling juxtapositions should attract attention, but scholarship also demands a self-reflexive attempt to counter this tendency. The more mundane or non-paradoxical changes also merit equal attention.

Moreover, given the concrete geo-cultural location of the centres of academic production, the globalization lens continues to be strongly Western in orientation. The West usually remains the major point of reference (implicit or explicit) even when the particular phenomenon being researched or the researchers involved are not Western.

It is not just a matter of West or non-West: the globalization literature is much less concerned than it ought to be with the different meanings and consequences that the term may have for social groups located differently along the axes of caste, class, gender, ethnicity, nationality and so on. Global flows may now be ubiquitous and to an extent multi-directional; but they continue to be strongly asymmetrical and unequal. To say that these flows are disjunctural or discordant or discrepant is not enough; explicit attention has to be paid to the specificities of the differences which mark different locales or groups.

While it is in the nature of the concept to stress the present moment, globalization must also pay close attention to the *historical trajectories* of the phenomena it studies. It is only when we know what went before that we can assess the nature and importance of what has come after globalization.

Finally, we need to pay adequate attention to the *concrete mechanisms* through which global flows take place and are sustained. It is often in these mechanisms that aspects of the continuity or the social embeddedness of institutions are visible. Ignoring them will therefore raise the risk of exaggerating change and its effects. Thus, while it may be true that images now have a truly global reach that is historically unprecedented, we also have to look carefully at the specific mechanisms through which this is achieved.

For example, even though they peddle globalized products, cable television operators need strong local roots to survive in the business. According to recent press reports, cable franchising in both Mumbai and Delhi has got mixed up in the turf battles among local gangs;[4] moreover, there are many other aspects of the supply chain which are inescapably local, such as the power supply or the sale and repair of equipment. These aspects of 'embeddedness' must be given due weightage when speaking of the global image.

QUESTIONS OF EVIDENCE

Many, perhaps most, of the problems mentioned in the preceding paragraphs are neither new nor wholly absent in the globalization literature: they are often mentioned in prefaces, introductions or conclusions. However, it is also true that the awareness of these shortcomings does not seem to have had any significant impact, and the globalization literature continues with business as usual.

One way of re-stating these problems is in terms of the researcher's vantage point and choice of subject. Perhaps my complaints are simply a product of the discord between two different types of perspectives, namely those which seek to tell the story of globalization as such, and those that approach it indirectly via its impact on some other primary subject such as a particular region, institution, or relationship. It seems almost inevitable that the scholar who seeks to study globalization will run the risk of exaggerating its importance or coherence, and, indeed, that she or he *ought* to do so. (In exactly the same way as the scholar interested in some other subject concentrates on that subject rather than on globalization.) Given that objects of inquiry are always partly constructed by the researcher, it cannot be asserted that an ethnic group or a region (for example) is somehow a more natural, self-evident or legitimate subject than globalization, or vice versa.

However, recognizing the claims to validity of different perspectives does not imply that they are all the same, nor does it absolve us from the responsibility of identifying the specific strengths and weaknesses of each. Indeed, the social scientific method demands that we strive to be self-reflexively aware of the weaknesses of the perspective we adopt and try to compensate for them. It is my contention that there has perhaps not been enough of this in the globalization literature. That is, the body of work which takes globalization itself as its object of study has not been sufficiently aware of the inevitable limitations of such a perspective when compared to others.

What is being attempted in this chapter, therefore, is an exercise in compensation: globalization is *not* the central subject here, rather it is being contextualized within a larger consideration of the spatiality of social identities, institutions and relations. Instead of asking questions about globalization as such, this chapter inquires about the changing spatial scale and coordinates of regional identities. It must be emphasized that this is a modest initial exercise designed to help clarify questions about what should and could count as legitimate evidence, the data that is available or may be generated, and the problems that arise in their interpretation.

The Geography of Regional Identity

One of the main methodological problems with most of the globalization literature is that it usually restricts itself to the data set that is most favourable to its basic premises. While this is not unusual in many kinds of social inquiry, it needs to be accompanied by an attempt to gauge the extent to which conclusions are influenced by the pre-selection of advantageous terrain.

Thus, if we begin with one of the most basic and common assumptions of the globalization thesis, namely, that the social world today is marked by much greater spatial movement and dynamism, the tendency in the literature is to substantiate this point by looking at groups and individuals *for whom this is already true*. This is perhaps unavoidable if the objective is to tell the story of globalization. What I am attempting here is to take up the much broader—and perhaps more long-lasting—issue associated with globalization, namely the thesis concerning the widening spatial ambit of social relationships and institutions. This is a part of my larger project on regional identities in the region known as the 'Bombay Karnatak', defined as the four districts—Bijapur, Belgaum, Dharwad and Uttar Kannada—of the British Indian Presidency of Bombay which became part of Karnataka in the linguistic reorganization of states after Independence. These four districts do not constitute a coherent region according to the Census definition, which is based largely on agro-climatic criteria.[5] However, it does seem to form a cultural region, the most interesting aspect of which is that it is a cusp culture—an overlap zone, or a hybrid (or mixed) cultural space where the transition from one 'pure' cultural identity to another can take place. Because it straddles the cultural division between 'north' and 'south' India, the Bombay Karnatak region marks both the southern boundary of northern culture as well as the northern boundary of southern culture.

What evidence can be produced in support of such an assertion? If we agree, for the moment, to ignore the inevitable fuzziness of terms like 'nothern culture', 'southern culture' and so on, we can begin with the informal evidence available in two major fields of culture, language and music. Even the rather bald initial definition of this region stated in the previous paragraph already provides a clue to the importance of language: these four districts were part of Bombay

Presidency, but the state's 'shadow lines' had to be re-drawn after independence to accommodate the southward pull exerted by 'Dravidian' Kannada against 'Indo-Aryan' Marathi. In music, on the other hand, the pull of the north is unmistakable, given that this small region located on the outskirts of the area of influence of the south Indian or Karnatak tradition, has produced so many giants of Hindustani classical music—including Bhimsen Joshi, Gangubai Hangal, Mallikarjun Mansur, Kumar Gandharva and Basavaraj Rajguru, besides the greats of earlier generations like Sawai Gandharva and Abdul Karim Khan.

Even on the basis of such anecdotal evidence, the probable status of the Bombay Karnatak as a cusp culture is of interest here because it highlights the spatial aspects of identity formation and deployment. In an in-between region, the changing geographical boundaries of the 'catchment area' from where the cultural raw materials for building identities are drawn are more noticeable precisely because they cut across other borders we are used to thinking in terms of. For example, when it was part of the Bombay Presidency and its major cultural and economic reference points were Pune and Mumbai, the cultural catchment area of the Bombay Karnatak would have been elongated in the north-westerly direction with a relatively smaller bulge southward. However, with inclusion in Karnataka, the region would change shape significantly, as it stretched southward towards the new state capital, Bangalore.

By mapping such shifts, we can hope to learn more about the concrete spatial dynamics of identity formation. Taken to its logical extreme, the globalization concept seems to argue that this kind of spatiality does not matter any more because, now, the raw materials for identity building can be sourced globally—maps lose much of their relevance when the whole world can be (and is) invoked from every corner of it. There is clearly some truth in this view, but also considerable exaggeration. The socio-spatial history of the Bombay Karnatak may provide a useful testing ground.

Obviously, such a project involves many preliminary steps,

including attempts to answer questions like the following: how and to what extent is it possible to make the transition from impressionistic information to 'hard' social scientific data where questions of identity formation are concerned? What sort of secondary data are available, and what are their strengths and limitations? Similarly, what sort of primary data could conceivably be collected, and in what aspects would they, in turn, be rich or poor? I have attempted to tackle these questions elsewhere, by looking at Census data on language, religion and migration. What I wish to do here is to move on to the next step of the argument, namely the tracking of the spatial spread of regional identities.

I begin with the rather conservative assumption that the geography of identity formation will be linked to the geography of social life itself. This allows us to specify the variables on which data need to be collected. Taking a very simple spatial view of the life process of the average social individual, we need to know where a person is born, where he/she grows up, is educated, finds employment, finds a marriage partner, and finally, where he/she spends the last phase of life. More accurately, what is needed is information on the *geographical spread* of these locations, for we are assuming that people find the materials for fashioning identities wherever they live. This is, of course, a truism and begs all the important questions; besides, it deals with only half the story, since the cultural resources for identity formation are always in circulation regardless of whether or not people are moving around. Nevertheless this may be a useful starting point for our investigation precisely because it drastically simplifies the task at hand—we are assuming that people build their identities solely with local cultural resources, and that only people move and cultural resources do not. This allows us to concentrate on the sort of evidence that is required to determine whether and to what degree cultural regions have been changed by globalization.

We need to address two dimensions: first, we need to track *changes across time* in the boundaries of the 'cultural watershed' from which identity-resources are drawn, both in terms of the life course of a single individual, and also in terms of inter-generational changes. Second, we need to monitor *differences across social groups and strata*, such as caste, class, community, rural/urban residence, and so on. Based on these parameters, a very simple survey was conducted to explore inter-generational and inter-group changes in the geography of identity formation. No elaborate sampling techniques were used, the criteria for selection of families being pragmatic ones, namely: a) residence in the Hubli-Dharwad region, and willingness to cooperate, which usually implied being able to get a personal reference/introduction from someone known to the family; b) families known to be large, and likely to produce data on at least three generations with significant numbers of mature adults (i.e., persons old enough to be employed and or married, and so on); c) families within the same broad range of economic status usually thought of as 'middle class'. The only criterion for stratification was by caste, with two families each being drawn from the Scheduled Tribes and Castes; the Lingayat community and Brahmins.

In each family, information was collected on three generations defined in relation to the respondent and his/her age:

Generation 1: Grandparents of respondents below fifty-five years (or else their parents) and their siblings;

Generation 2: All the children of those in Generation 1;

Generation 3: All the children of those in Generation 2.

For each person in each generation of each family,[6] information was collected on the following variables, defined as the distance from a pre-selected geographical spot taken to be the centre of the putative cultural region being studied:

1. Place of birth and/or family residence (the latter if the two were different);

2. Place(s) of education;

3. Place(s) of employment;

4. Place of residence of spouse immediately before marriage;

5. Place of last residence (for deceased persons) or current residence.

Where more than one place was involved, the place farthest from the family home where at least one year was spent was taken. Thus, the exact variable measured in these cases was the maximum distance from the family home of places of education, employment and so on.

The overall intention of this mini survey was to study variations in the geographical spread (relative to the family home) of places of education, employment, spousal residence and current/last residence across generations, and across caste groups. The detailed findings are presented in Tables A through D at the end of this chapter; the most important findings are discussed below.

Table 1 presents the main variations across time, or the three loosely defined 'generations' of each family. The spatial spread is divided into five divisions, starting with the micro-region (defined as a radius of up to 100 km around the family home); the meso-region (100 to 500 km); macro-region (500–1,000 km); the national level (more than 1,000 km, but within the nation); and, finally, the blanket category of the international level which includes all locations outside the nation regardless of distance. Table 1 concentrates solely on inter-generational differences, with all castes being clubbed.

Overall, the most salient point being made in Table 1 is that people in this region—even when the notion of 'people' is confined to the 'middle classes'—don't really seem to have spread out beyond their inherited micro-environment, defined as a radius of about a hundred kilometres around the family residence. Even in the third generation (henceforth G3), there is a remarkable concentration of people within the micro-region, and the percentages of respondents who have not gone beyond this sphere is 81 per cent for education, 77 per cent for seeking spouses, and 64 per cent for last/current residence. Employment is the only area where there is a major change, with the proportion staying within the micro-region having declined to only 58 per cent in G3 compared to 94 per cent in G1. Thus, with the exception of employment, around two-thirds or more of respondents seem still to be confined to the 100-km micro-region.

Analysing the spread that has occurred, it is clear that most of it is

TABLE 1
Variable Profiles Across Generations, Clubbing All Castes

	0-100 km	100-500 km	500-1000 km	1000+ km	Abroad	Total
EDUCATION						
GEN-1	97	3	0	0	0	100 (35)
GEN-2	87	9	4	0	0	100 (70)
GEN-3	81	7	6	3	2	100 (175)
ALL	85	7	5	2	1	100 (280)
EMPLOYMENT						
GEN-1	94	3	3	0	0	100 (35)
GEN-2	74	13	9	0	1	100 (70)
GEN-3	58	27	7	3	4	100 (162)★
ALL	67	20	7	2	3	100 (267)★
SPOUSAL HOME						
GEN-1	97	3		0	0	100 (35)
GEN-2	78	17	1	3	0	100 (69)★
GEN-3	77	16	5	1	0	100 (154)★
ALL	80	15	4	2	0	100 (258)
LAST / CURRENT RESIDENCE						
GEN-1	91	6	3	0	0	100 (35)
GEN-2	81	13	4	1	0	100 (70)
GEN-3	64	22	9	2	3	100 (175)
ALL	72	18	7	2	2	100 (280)

Note: Cells show percentage shares; number of persons is shown in brackets in the Total column. Star (★) indicates some persons were underage and or unemployed/ unmarried. *Source:* Compiled from Field Data.

confined to the meso-region, or a radius of 500 km. Thus, the percentage of respondents who have moved out of the micro- into the meso-region in G3 is 7 per cent for education; 27 per cent for employment; 16 per cent for seeking spouses and 22 per cent for their last/current residence. Similar figures for the macro-region, or a radius of 1,000 km, drop down to the single digits, ranging from 5 per cent for spousal home to 9 per cent for current/last residence. Finally, it is interesting to look at the 'Abroad' column, which shows that this is entirely a G3 phenomenon,[7] and is as yet of negligible numerical importance, ranging from zero for spousal home to a maximum of 4 per cent for employment.

Table 1 highlighted the shifts across generations for the sample as a whole, regardless of caste variations; Table 2 below provides an overview of the differences across castes, this time ignoring variations across generations. It is immediately obvious from Table 2 that there are very major differences across three caste groups in this broadly same (middle) class sample—most of the spatial spread is attributable to the Brahmin community. The respondents from the Lingayat community seem quite remarkably concentrated within the micro-region, though this may be an aberration due to the particular characteristics of the two families in the sample.[8] The SC/ST caste group seems slightly more mobile than the Lingayats, but this is largely in the last/current residence category, and even in this category does not go beyond the macro-region of 1,000 km.

The Brahmin rows in Table 2 are quite striking in that all the cells have non-zero values, with the sole exception being the 'Abroad' column for the spousal home.[9] Spread seems the most for the employment category—indeed this is what is behind the all-caste averages, for the other castes do not show anywhere near the kind of mobility in employment as the Brahmins. It is somewhat surprising though that spousal home should show more spread than education, and this would perhaps need further investigation. Nevertheless, even among Brahmins, the vast majority are confined to the meso-region, with relatively few venturing beyond it in any category. As for the 'Abroad' category, this is almost entirely a G3 phenomenon even for the Brahmins. It is interesting to note, though, that it is represented in all spheres except spousal home, though the numbers involved are as yet miniscule. Another noteworthy feature is that there is not much difference between the national and the international levels—once a person is outside the macro-region of 1,000 km radius, he/she is almost as likely to be abroad as within the country.

TABLE 2
Caste Profiles By Variable, Clubbing All Generations

	0-100 km	100-500 km	500-1000 km	1000+ km	Abroad	Total
SC / ST						
Education	95	4	1	0	0	100 (73)
Employment	94	5	2	0	0	100 (63)★
Spousal Home	93	7	0	0	0	100 (60)★
Residence	80	16	4	0	0	100 (73)
LINGAYAT						
Education	100	0	0	0	0	100 (74)
Employment	91	8	0	0	1	100 (74)
Spousal Home	99	1	0	0	0	100 (74)
Residence	92	8	0	0	0	100 (74)
BRAHMIN						
Education	71	12	10	5	3	100 (133)
Employment	41	35	14	5	5	100 (130)★
Spousal Home	63	27	7	3	0	100 (124)★
Residence	56	23	12	4	5	100 (133)
ALL CASTES						
Education	85	7	5	2	1	100 (280)
Employment	67	20	7	2	3	100 (267)★
Spousal Home	80	15	4	2	0	100 (258)★
Residence	72	18	7	2	2	100 (280)

Note: Cells show percentage shares; number of persons is shown in brackets in the Total column. Star (★) indicates some persons were underage and or unemployed/ unmarried. *Source:* Compiled from Field Data.

What do these data reveal (and conceal) about the spatial aspects of identity? In this particular illustration, for example, the data tell us that the geographical spread of the middle classes in this region remains tightly localized for the most part, though there seems to be a trend towards greater dispersion. Even in the third generation, comparatively few family members venture forth beyond the macro-region (500 km radius), and when they do, they are just as likely to go abroad as to a different region within the country. Most important, even among the middle classes, there are very major inter-caste differences in mobility, with the Brahmins seeming to be much more mobile than the two other caste groups considered. It has to be emphasized, of course, that these are merely illustrative data and do not constitute a substantial research study.

However, even at this illustrative level, such data remain silent on a number of issues. Since they only convey abstracted measures of distance, they do not tell us about the geographic areas of spread—i.e., in which specific directions the 'cultural watershed' is extending; they offer absolutely no information on the contexts in which the decisions to move out or stay back were taken, to what degrees they were forced and/or voluntary, and so on; finally, the data give us no clues about the perceived worth of specific movements (are those who go abroad admired or despised? is getting a spouse from a far off place seen as a triumph or a disaster? and so on).

Although they can never substitute for sensitive qualitative accounts, such data—when properly representative of the spectrum of social groups and locations in a given region—do have the immense value of providing a basic spatial benchmark against which further speculative information or arguments on globalization can be framed. This kind of survey data offer the hope of transcending the unavoidable limitations of scale for qualitative research methods, while at the same time providing much more (and more accurately directed) data than is available from macro sources like the Census. Because of this, such data can act as an invaluable balancing factor—as intellectual ballast, so to speak, which may help prevent attractive but extravagant arguments regarding globalization from blowing us off our feet.

Globalization-as-transnationalism and identity formation

The argument of the preceding two parts has consciously avoided direct reference to globalization as an issue or process that may also be present in the contexts being studied. If we return to this question now, what would change in our approach and what additional/ alternative types of data would we look for?

The first step would be to specify the implications of the deliberately restrictive assumptions with which I began, namely the assumption that the geographical spread of social life would define the cultural watershed relevant for identity construction. This is clearly an untenable assumption for it completely ignores the fact that each place/location is not simply a self-contained spot on the map but also has various cultural winds blowing through it carrying materials from distant places and contexts. To thus assume away the impact of communication media is to simplify the picture to the point of falsification. A conventional study of globalization in this context might begin to rectify this by looking for anecdotal evidence of international influences.

Going back in history, it could be said, for example, that this region has been affected by the global trade networks created by the Vijayanagar empire in the sixteenth century. These trade routes involved the movement of people and commodities from places like Burma, China, Java, Sumatra, Bali, and Malaya in the east, and Hormuz, the Mediterranean coast and Portugal in the West. The Dharwad micro-region was on the land route from the ports of the Konkan (Goa, Basrur, Honnavar, Bhatkal and Mangalore) to the Vijayanagar capital at Hampi. In fact, a Portuguese historian notes the presence of the 'Ruler of Bankapur' (a small principality in the south of the contemporary district of Dharwad) at the February 1548 talks between the Vijayanagar monarchy and the ambassadors of the Portuguese ruler D.Joao de Castro (Lima Cruz 1998:26-27). More than four centuries later, an ethnographic study of a village near Dharwad notes that (in the early 1960s) villagers were familiar with American wheat, Dutch fertilizer and milk products, European medicines and the impact of British industry in general (Ishwaran 1968:15-16). The region has also witnessed Swiss and German Christian missionary activity since at least the last quarter of the nineteenth century, the Basel and Kittel missions having been active here. This could be followed up through the Censuses (migration data indicating the presence of foreign-born persons in the region) and, of course, the archives of Christian institutions themselves. The strong Muslim presence in the region for several centuries and the proximity of the coast would point to Arab influence via trade and the Haj pilgrimages. On a different plane, one could point to the undoubted influence of satellite television and the cultural impact of such historically unprecedented availability of largely Western but also global images and world views. A particularly telling anecdotal illustration of this impact is provided by the fact that, in a nationwide Michael Jackson lookalike contest organized some years ago by a soft drinks company (in preparation for his aborted first tour of India), the runner-up was a young man from Hubli.

One could go on in this vein to outline the manner in which a study of globalization in the Bombay Karnatak could proceed, but the essential point I wish to make is different. What I would like to draw attention to is the *minimal overlap* between the sorts of evidence discussed above and the sorts of evidence presented in the previous sections on the spatial aspects of the regional identity associated with the Bombay Karnatak. The point is made even sharper when we consider specific evidence of the intergenerational family survey.

In the data on the intergenerational family survey, the main interest would be in the 'Abroad' column, which may be further refined or expanded, while the rest of the columns would be largely irrelevant. One would therefore not notice the curious relation of competition or substitution between the metropolitan centres within the nation and the world at large. In the same fashion, by concentrating on satellite television, one would miss the intermediate stages through which a national audience was created first through radio broadcasts of Hindi film music, and then for Hindi films themselves. (Hubli-Dharwad had as many as fourteen cinema halls in the 1970s, when a north Indian city of comparable size would at most have had six or seven.)

It is important to emphasize that these biases would enter into studies of globalization not due to any fault of the researchers (or the details of their methodology) but by virtue of the very way in which the inquiry is structured. If one sets out to look for globalization it is usually impossible to avoid finding it, and most often the systemic push of the various institutional logics involved (Ph.D. dissertation requirements, funding agency guidelines, or the editorial policies of journals, for example) will ensure that it is accorded the role of the protagonist in whatever story that may be told.

However, one should not overstate or mis-state the argument being made here. It is perfectly true that what is numerically or quantitatively in the 'majority' need not necessarily be the most dynamic or the most important feature in a given social context. Dynamic processes and actors who have history on their side, so to speak, are surely more important than others that may be more numerous but relatively inert. However, this possibility needs to be *demonstrated*, not simply assumed. Statistically dominant phenomena may (often for that very reason) be 'boring' or unattractive, particularly to the researcher looking for interesting paradoxes and curiosities; but this does not mean that they have lost their weight or influence. One must therefore provide explicit justification for according *priority* to the new, the paradoxical and the changing over the unchanging and the conventional. This is what studies of globalization are usually unable to do because of the way in which they are structured.

Globalization and hindutva

Finally, it may be useful to consider the interaction between globalization and another major force that has been altering the social landscape of India, namely hindutva. As seen in Chapter Four, hindutva appears to be diametrically opposed to globalization and its tendency to accentuate the unique particularity of the nation as a sacred space.

At first glance, there seems little doubt that globalization is a contrary tendency—it seems to undermine the particularity of places, subordinating them to a universalized logic. The orientalist version of this tendency has been labelled 'moral commensuration', a practice whereby Western metropolitan places are assigned 'a kind of export value: whatever is good or bad about places at home is shipped out and assigned comparable virtue or vice abroad' (Said 1993:79). However, the contemporary equivalent for globalization seems (usually, but not always) to move in the reverse direction: non-Western (Third World) places are compared to some Western place (which acts as a norm), and are thus assigned a new ideological value.[10] In effect, this kind of moral commensuration 'equalizes' places and seeks to underplay differences rather than to accentuate them.

More generally, theoretical prognoses of the development of capitalism from Marx onwards have pointed to the universalizing tendencies of capital. In spatial terms, this expresses itself in the process of de-territorialization, the uprooting and enforced 'portability' of all forms of social life captured by capital, or 'the disembedding of social relations'. This is the process rendered familiar by the literature on the 'restructuring of capital', 'flexible accumulation' and 'post-Fordism'.[11] Industries turn nomadic in the search for the most profitable location; production processes are broken up and subcontracted globally; innovations in telecommunications enable certain industries (like computer software) to engage in 'space-less' production—i.e., without a single, specific spatial location in the conventional sense. (Satellite links enable software engineers located in far-flung corners of the globe to participate simultaneously in production, while the product itself exists only in the 'cyberspace' of electronic storage devices.) The basic outcome of such a conquest of space is a profound indifference towards its specificities. Thus, the spatial consequences of the economic logic of contemporary capitalism include the dilution of nation-specific production into a more anonymous globalized process (Deshpande 1993b).

However, recent research has also demonstrated that the alleged conquest of space is far from complete and is in any case a rather uneven and contradictory process. These researches build on the insight reported more than two decades ago, namely that although modern societies are defined by processes of deterritorialization, '*what they deterritorialize with one hand, they reterritorialize with the other*' (Deleuze & Guattari [1972]1977:257, original emphasis). The process of reterritorialization takes many forms, but two are specially common. First, there is the simple refusal of archaic territorial entities to go away, and, indeed, an increase in their mass appeal. An excellent example is the nation, which, in defiance of widespread expectations about the erosion of national identities, continues to command the often fanatical loyalty of large numbers. The second, more complex form of reterritorialization is an integral part of the process of globalization itself, namely the cultivation and deepening of spatial specificity, but within a framework where this is subordinated to the overall logic of globalization. Obvious examples are the tourism industry or the media, which foster and even invent specificity as 'authentic exoticism', but only in order to offer up these exotica in a standardized, pre-packaged form to global consumers of cultural difference such as affluent tourists, or cinema and television audiences.[12]

This latter tendency has caught the attention of social researchers trying to account for the striking fact that globalization is *accompanied by* the growth of particularistic cultural identities of all kinds. Across the globe today, 'ascriptive' cultural identities of all sorts (i.e., identities acquired by birth rather than choice or training)—including those based on religion, ethnicity, nationality, language, or region—are enjoying an unprecedented revival even as the processes of globalization are simultaneously intensified. It has been tempting, therefore, to speculate on a possible causal link between the two processes, in the form of the broad thesis that globalization produces a sort of 'identity anxiety'. Individuals and groups seek to assuage this anxiety by reasserting their particularistic or 'local' identities. Economic globalism produces—indeed, even requires—cultural parochialism as its own antidote and precondition. Religious revival seems to be a common reaction, as demonstrated by the remarkable revitalization of Catholic, Protestant, Jewish, Islamic, Hindu and Buddhist fundamentalisms of various kinds in widely differing contexts (Beyer 1990).

It is clear, therefore, that globalization and hindutva impact on each other in contradictory as well as complementary ways, not to speak of ways that may go beyond this dichotomy. Their mutual involvements cannot be understood in terms of a simple or unidimensional model. One important aspect of this mutual impact is the globalization of hindutva itself, that is, the globalization of its congregations and constituencies. The emergence of 'non-resident *hindutva*' provides an instance where the 'portability' (or the cross-cultural transmission) and the 'changelessness' (or cultural rootedness) of religious identities are *simultaneously* intensified. Today, when the world is witness to more and more such encounters—involving both collusions and collisions—between the local and the globalized faces of ethnicity (Appadurai 1990), the net outcome cannot be predicted.

TABLE A
Distribution of Distance from Family Home to Place of Education
By Caste Group and Generations

	0-100 km	100-500 km	500-1000 km	1000+ km	Abroad	Total
SC/ST						
GEN-1	100 (13)		0	0	0	100 (13)
GEN-2	100 (23)		0	0	0	100 (23)
GEN-3	89.2 (33)	8.1 (3)	1 (2.7)	0	0	100 (37)
ALL	94.5 (69)	4.1 (3)	1 (1.4)	0	0	100 (73)
LINGAYAT						
GEN-1	100 (9)	0	0	0	0	100 (9)
GEN-2	100 (16)	0	0	0	0	100 (16)
GEN-3	100 (49)	0	0	0	0	100 (49)
ALL	100 (74)	0	0	0	0	100 (74)
BRAHMIN						
GEN-1	92.3 (12)	7.7 (1)	0	0	0	100 (13)
GEN-2	71.0 (22)	19.4 (6)	9.7 (3)	0	0	100 (31)
GEN-3	67.4 (60)	10.1 (9)	11.2 (10)	6.7 (6)	4.5 (4)	100 (89)
ALL	70.7 (94)	12.0 (16)	9.8 (13)	4.5 (6)	3.0 (4)	100 (133)
ALL CASTES						
GEN-1	97.1 (34)	2.9 (1)	0	0	0	100 (35)
GEN-2	87.1 (61)	8.6 (6)	4.3 (3)	0	0	100 (70)
GEN-3	81.1 (142)	6.9 (12)	6.3 (11)	3.4 (6)	2.3 (4)	100 (175)
ALL	84.6 (237)	6.8 (19)	5.0 (14)	2.1 (6)	1.4 (4)	100 (280)

Note: Cells show percentage shares, with number of persons in brackets. Where more than one place of residence is involved, the farthest place with at least one year's stay is taken. All distances are in kilometres from Hubli-Dharwad, or the family home.
Source: Compiled from Field Data.

TABLE B

Distribution of Distance from Family Home to Place of Employment

By Caste Group and Generations

	0-100 km	100-500 km	500-1000 km	1000 + km	Abroad	Total
SC/ST						
GEN-1	100 (13)	0	0	0	0	100 (13)
GEN-2	100 (23)	0	0	0	0	100 (23)
GEN-3	85.2 (23)	11.1 (3)	3.7 (1)	0	0	100 (27)★
ALL	93.7 (59)	4.8 (3)	1.6 (1)	0	0	100 (63)★
LINGAYAT						
GEN-1	100 (9)	0	0	0	0	100 (9)
GEN-2	87.5 (14)	12.5 (2)	0	0	0	100 (16)
GEN-3	89.8 (44)	8.2 (4)	0	0	2.0 (1)	100 (49)
ALL	90.5 (67)	8.1 (6)	0	0	1.4 (1)	100 (74)
BRAHMIN						
GEN-1	84.6 (11)	7.7 (1)	7.7 (1)	0	0	100 (13)
GEN-2	48.4 (15)	22.6 (7)	19.4 (6)	0	3.2 (1)	100 (31)
GEN-3	31.4 (27)	43.0 (37)	12.8 (11)	6.7 (6)	7.0 (6)	100 (86)★
ALL	40.8 (53)	34.6 (45)	13.8 (18)	4.5 (6)	5.4 (7)	100 (130)★
ALL CASTES						
GEN-1	94.3 (33)	2.9 (1)	2.9 (1)	0	0	100 (35)
GEN-2	74.3 (52)	12.9 (9)	8.6 (6)	0	1.4 (1)	100 (70)
GEN-3	58.0 (94)	27.2 (44)	7.4 (12)	3.4 (6)	4.3 (7)	100 (162)★
ALL	67.0 (179)	20.2 (54)	7.1 (19)	2.1 (6)	3.0 (8)	100 (267)★

Note: Cells show percentage shares, with number of persons in brackets. Where more than one place of residence is involved, the farthest place with at least one year's stay is taken. All distances are in kilometres from Hubli-Dharwad, or the family home. Star (★) indicates that not all persons were employed. *Source:* Compiled from Field Data.

175

TABLE C
Distribution of Distance from Family Home to Spousal Family Home
By Caste Group and Generations

	0-100 km	100-500 km	500-1000 km	1000+ km	Abroad	Total
SC/ST						
GEN-1	100 (13)	0	0	0	0	100 (13)
GEN-2	91.3 (21)	8.7 (2)	0	0	0	100 (23)
GEN-3	91.7 (22)	8.3 (2)	0	0	0	100 (24)★
ALL	93.3 (56)	6.7 (4)	0	0	0	100 (60)★
LINGAYAT						
GEN-1	100 (9)	0	0	0	0	100 (9)
GEN-2	100 (16)	0	0	0	0	100 (16)
GEN-3	98.0 (48)	2.0 (1)	0	0	0	100 (49)
ALL	98.6 (73)	1.4 (1)	0	0	0	100 (74)
BRAHMIN						
GEN-1	92.3 (12)	7.7 (1)	0	0	0	100 (13)
GEN-2	56.7 (17)	33.3 (10)	3.3 (1)	6.7 (2)	0	100 (30)★
GEN-3	60.5 (49)	27.2 (22)	9.9 (8)	2.5 (2)	0	100 (81)★
ALL	62.9 (78)	26.6 (33)	7.3 (9)	3.2 (4)	0	100 (124)★
ALL CASTES						
GEN-1	97.1 (34)	2.9 (1)	0	0	0	100 (35)
GEN-2	78.3 (54)	17.4 (12)	1.4 (1)	2.9 (2)	0	100 (69)★
GEN-3	77.3 (119)	16.2 (25)	5.2 (8)	1.3 (2)	0	100 (154)★
ALL	80.2 (207)	14.7 (38)	3.5 (9)	1.6 (4)	0	100 (258)★s

Note: Cells show percentage shares, with number of persons in brackets. Where more than one place of residence is involved, the farthest place with at least one year's stay is taken. All distances are in kilometres from Hubli-Dharwad, or the family home. Stat (*) indicates, not all persons were married. *Source:* Compiled from Field Data.

TABLE D
Distribution of Distance from Family Home to Place of Current or Last Residence
By Caste Group and Generations

	0-100 km	100-500 km	500-1000 km	1000 +km	Abroad	Total
SC/ST						
GEN-1	92.3 (12)	7.7 (1)	0	0	0	100 (13)
GEN-2	95.7 (22)	4.3 (1)	0	0	0	100 (23)
GEN-3	64.9 (24)	27.0 (10)	8.1 (3)	0	0	100 (37)
ALL	79.5 (58)	16.4 (12)	4.1 (3)	0	0	100 (73)
LINGAYAT						
GEN-1	100 (9)	0	0	0	0	100 (9)
GEN-2	93.8 (15)	6.3 (1)	0	0	0	100 (16)
GEN-3	89.8 (44)	10.2 (5)	0	0	0	100 (49)
ALL	91.9 (68)	8.1 (6)	0	0	0	100 (74)
BRAHMIN						
GEN-1	84.6 (11)	7.7 (1)	7.7 (1)	0	0	100 (13)
GEN-2	64.5 (20)	22.6 (7)	9.7 (3)	3.2 (1)	0	100 (31)
GEN-3	49.4 (44)	25.8 (23)	13.5 (12)	4.5 (4)	6.7 (6)	100 (89)
ALL	56.4 (75)	23.3 (31)	12.0 (16)	3.8 (5)	4.5 (6)	100 (133)
ALL CASTES						
GEN-1	91.4 (32)	5.7 (2)	2.9 (1)	0	0	100 (35)
GEN-2	81.4 (57)	12.9 (9)	4.3 (3)	1.4 (1)	0	100 (70)
GEN-3	64.0 (112)	21.7 (38)	8.6 (15)	2.3 (4)	3.4 (6)	100 (175)
ALL	71.8 (201)	17.5 (49)	6.8 (19)	1.8 (5)	2.1 (6)	100 (280)

Note: Cells show percentage shares, with number of persons in brackets. Where more than one place of residence is involved, the farthest place with at least one year's stay is taken. All distances are in kilometres from Hubli-Dharwad, or the family home.
Source: Compiled from Field Data.

Notes

1. Squinting at Society

1. To establish this point, ethnomethodologist Harold Garfinkel conducted a controversial set of 'breaching experiments' in which his graduate students at the University of California in Los Angeles deliberately breached the implicit social contract by refusing to use their commonsense and requiring their unsuspecting interlocutors to explain themselves 'fully'. These experiments had to be quickly abandoned because they turned mundane conversations into traumatic events and brought even close relationships to the brink of breakdown.

2. This in essence is the model of nationalism attributed to Bankim Chattopadhyaya in Partha Chatterjee's well-known work (1986). Variations on this basic theme can be found strewn all over the history of Indian nationalism even to this day.

3. The phrase in quotes is the title of a famous book by Daniel Lerner.

4. It is interesting to note that M.N. Srinivas began his career in India in the 1950s with the opposite view—that is, by advocating the cause of participant observation as a much neglected method contrary to the popularity of survey research (Srinivas 1994:14-18). At the end of the century, the shoe would certainly seem to be on the other foot. It would not be easy to cite even five survey-based or quantitatively-oriented studies that have had a major impact on Indian sociology during the last fifty years.

5. I do not mean to imply that anthropology has no contribution to

make in development, or that involvement in state initiatives is always a good thing. We are now much wiser on both counts. I am only trying to understand why—according to the *then prevailing notions* of what disciplines were about and what development entailed and so on—the outcomes that would have been predicted by the social logic of institutions failed to materialize.

6. Satish Saberwal, himself a maverick figure among sociologists, has a very perceptive essay on this theme (Saberwal 1999). To the best of my knowledge, this is the only extended treatment of the subject by any major scholar.

2. Mapping a Distinctive Modernity

1. Historian Cyril Black has written that in ancient Latin, modern was 'a term denoting the quality of a contemporary era' (Black 1966:5). Raymond Williams also notes that the earliest English meanings of the word 'were nearer our *contemporary*, in the sense of something existing now, just now' (Williams 1983:208-9, original emphasis).

2. Original emphasis, abbreviations expanded; see also Williams 1989:31-2.

3. These two factors also contributed to the emergence of the multilateral institutional complex built around the United Nations, which also undertook research on modernization and allied issues in the Third World.

4. Personal communication from Redfield to Singer, May 1956, quoted in Singer (1972:8).

5. Apart from Cohn's essay cited above, overviews of early work on Indian society and culture are to be found in Kopf 1969, Mandelbaum 1970, Madan 1995 (Ch.5: 'Images of India in American Anthropology'), Srinivas and Panini 1973, and Saberwal 1986.

6. For example, Louis Dumont felt that the strong desire for change and the state-sponsored drive towards it may force researchers to be less vigilant about the *continuities* (or lack of change) in society

(Dumont 1964:10). Similar sentiments were echoed by Ramakrishna Mukherjee in his complaint that the 'modernizers' among Indian sociologists neglected the 'null hypothesis' of 'no change' (Mukherjee 1979:52). An interesting early discussion of the links among, and the implications of, the community and village studies research, the state-sponsored tendency towards social engineering, and the heavy involvement of Western, particularly American, researchers and institutions is to be found in Saran (1958:1026-32).

7. As Dean Tipps has pointed out, anthropologists—the very people who knew the most about the Third World societies that modernization theory was setting out to study—were typically the least enthusiastic about it. (Tipps 1973:207, see also footnote 4.) This could also be due to the fundamental orientation of classical anthropology towards pre-modern societies, such that modernization seems anthithetical to the very *raison d'etre* of the discipline.

8. George Rosen speaks of the Indian government alternating between 'great sensitivity' and 'undue respect' for foreign scholars and provides useful details (Rosen 1985:52-54). For example: Douglas Ensminger (the American rural sociologist and Ford Foundation consultant in India in the 1950s and 1960s, closely associated with the Community Development Programme) had the kind of direct access to Prime Minister Nehru and the Planning Commission that would have been envied by Indian sociologists, though some economists enjoyed similar status. And A.K. Saran points out that after independence, local scholars may, on the one hand, be enabled to ask uncomfortable questions about the desirability of foreign collaboration; but, on the other hand, they may also become much more hospitable to foreign influences once freed of the moral burden of subject status (Saran 1958:1028-9, 1031-2).

9. One reason, perhaps, why Indian sociology has sometimes looked like a tired discipline (Deshpande 1994).

10. In a brief later article Srinivas returns to this theme while discussing 'the oft-heard comment that Indians do not have a sense of contradiction, or that it does not have the same emotional and other

implications for them as it has for Westerners' (1971b:155; page references in this paragraph are to this work). After giving further examples of the Indian talent for tolerating the contradiction between modern and traditional world views (including Nehru—publicly contemptuous of astrology, yet pressing his daughter to get a proper horoscope made for his new-born grandson, pp.155-6), Srinivas distinguishes sources of contradiction found in all cultures (such as role conflict)) from those likely to be peculiar to developing societies (such as the compulsion to appear modernized and the very rapid pace of change). He wonders if 'the urge to consistency may become stronger' with further social change, thus accentuating the feeling of contradiction, which, in turn, 'may be accompanied by increased mental illness' (p. 158).

11. An interesting example is provided by K.N. Raj, a leading Indian economist closely involved with development planning, who recalls that Gulzarilal Nanda, the minister in charge of planning, twice postponed the signing of the First Five Year Plan, insisting on a numerologically auspicious day (Raj 1997:108).

12. But too much must not be made of such differences. After all, they hold only for the early stage of modernization studies up to the 1960s; there is every reason to presume that anthropological accounts of Third World modernization grew in sophistication over time. Moreover, comparisons of this sort need to consider carefully further questions of detail: are the Lerner or Inkeles-Smith type of multi-country survey-based studies really comparable with Srinivas' solo ethnography? and so on.

13. A similar situation may conceivably have existed in the South and Central American nations, which were formally independent long before the decolonization of Asia and Africa. A different but well-known instance is that of the Carribbean colonies which, between the 1920s and the 1960s, had already produced a glittering galaxy of writers and intellectuals, including Aimé Césaire, Frantz Fanon, Edouard Glissant, Walter Rodney, Eric Williams, C.L.R. James, and W. Arthur Lewis. But the presence of a sizeable 'Westernized' local

academic establishment (even if colonial in origin and design) is in all probability peculiar to India. My ignorance of other Third World histories prevents a more informed statement.

14. The last chapter of *Social Change in Modern India*, 'Some thoughts on the study of one's own society', is on this very subject: 'One of the things that strikes me as I look back on the reception accorded my work outside my country is the repeated reference to my being an Indian sociologist engaged in the study of my own society.' (1971a:147.) Srinivas goes on to note that while opinion was divided on whether this was an asset or a liability, his Indianness was invariably remarked upon. For a recent reformulation of his views on this subject, see Srinivas 1996.

15. Srinivas himself seems to prefer Westernization to modernization. But the reasons he provides are curious: he believes that modernization implies a value-judgement regarding ultimate goals, which social scientists are unable to endorse or reject, whereas Westernization is a more neutral term (Srinivas 1971a:50-52).

16. For example, Rajadhyaksha 1993, and Prasad 1998a.

17. See, for example, the collections edited by Uberoi 1996, and John and Nair 1998.

18. Such a comparative perspective must also, as Mariza Peirano points out, prevent our interest in other Third World countries being restricted to the desire to counter Western theories or models, such that, for example, Brazil exists for Indian sociology only in so far as it is the source of dependency theory (Peirano 1991).

19. A phrase attributed to Ashis Nandy by Banuri (1990:95).

3. The Nation as an Imagined Economy

1 . For example, Emile Durkheim insisted that social institutions were *emergent* phenomena, always greater than the sum of their parts, not only founded on shared beliefs, norms and values, but also themselves 'collective representations' to a greater or lesser degree. From a

different philosophical starting point, the social constructionists and symbolic interactionists came to the same conclusion: to paraphrase W.I. Thomas' famous dictum, whatever people believe to be real will always produce real consequences, regardless of whether it is, in fact, real.

2. For example, Louis Dumont's idiosyncratic reflections on 'communalism and nationalism' (1964), or M.N. Srinivas' slightly earlier musings on 'the problem of Indian unity'.

3. Of these, two are particularly relevant (and non-controversial) in the non-West: the 'lonely, bilingual intelligentsias' (Anderson 1983:127), created by imperialism in colonized countries that are alienated from their own society and denied an equal share in imperial society, thus being forced to imagine the nation as their legitimate domain; and the pre-modern states (mostly monarchies) that try to (or are forced to) legitimize themselves in the modern fashion by retrospectively inventing nations which they then claim to represent. In the second edition of his work, Anderson has added a chapter on the census, the map and the museum as additional devices that help to construct the idea of the nation and to supply it with mnemonic aids (Anderson 1991).

4. Of course, this is a rather broad and oversimple characterization. At no point was the Indian nation synonymous with an imagined national economy: the figure of Mother India, despite the ubiquitous references to her poverty, is surely much more than an economic metaphor. Nor are the stages identified above anything other than very general and partial labels for an obviously more complex and multivocal history. Despite these shortcomings, however, this description does serve a heuristic purpose: it helps us to track one crucial strand among the many that combine to make the imagined community that is the Indian nation.

5. For a more detailed discussion, see Deshpande 1993, pp. 14-16.

6. An extended discussion is available in Deshpande 1993, pp. 20-25.

7. Here is what Justice Ranade had to say: 'The agitation for political rights may bind the various nationalities of India together for a time.

The community of interests may cease when these rights are achieved. But the commercial union of the various nationalities, once established, will never cease to exist. Commercial and industrial activity is, therefore, a bond of very strong union and is, therefore, a mighty factor in the formation of a great Indian nation.' (Quoted in Chandra 1966:69.)

8. Here Gandhi, though he offers a different solution, is quite close to the spirit of Marx in opposing the reification and exploitation that generalized commodity production brings with it.

9. It now seems to me that a more accurate description of this situation might be that those who are labelled as 'anti-development' are made to carry the burden of an 'excessive' cultural identity, while the modernist forces lay claim to a more culturally abstract (and in this sense understated) identity. But this line of argument needs to be considered more carefully in the complex context of an identity politics 'before its time', i.e., during the Nehru era. In a certain sense, contemporary anti-developmentalist and anti-modernist positions (Ashis Nandy's would be the best known in India) can be seen as trying to self-consciously reclaim this 'excessively cultural' (or essentialist) identity and invest it with a positive critical-moral charge.

4. *Hindutva and its Spatial Strategies*

1. The phrase quoted forms the subtitle of Soja 1989; some other works that treat social space in an innovative way include: Lefebvre 1991, Bourdieu 1984 (specially Part II, Chs. 2 & 3), De Certeau 1980 (specially Part III, Chs.VII–IX), Tuan 1977, Sack 1986, and Harvey 1989.

2. For different perspectives on these and related issues, see, for example, Anderson 1991, Smith 1986 (specially Ch. 8), and Wallerstein & Balibar 1991.

3. 'Instantly recognizable, everywhere visible, the logo-map penetrated

deep into the popular imagination, forming a powerful emblem for the anticolonial nationalisms being born.' (Anderson 1991:173.)

4. Compare Basu et al. (1993:1, fn). This is obviously an imprecise definition in that it does not recognize the many distinct (and sometimes contrary) tendencies contained within the same overall phenomenon. However, it will suffice for the purposes of this chapter.

5. Jawaharlal Nehru is a good example, as several passages from his *Autobiography* (Nehru 1985) or *The Discovery of India* (Nehru 1946) attest.

6. Partha Chatterjee's well-known account, for example, constructs the 'moment of departure' of Indian nationalist discourse in terms of the Bankim model: modern (Western) science and technology plus traditional (Indian) dharma and culture (Chatterjee 1986).

7. For the purposes of this chapter, communalism involves both (a) the pursuit of political goals through the open or hidden appeal to religious sentiment and/or identities; and (b) the exploitation of this sentiment to exclude other religious groups and to cultivate hostility towards them.

8. I am restricting myself here to a single work by a single author, 'Swatantraya Veer' V.D. Savarkar and his pamphlet, *Hindutva*. This pamphlet is contained in volume VI ('Hindu Rashtra Darshan') of the *Sampurna Savarkar Wangmaya*, the collected works of Savarkar, published (and partially translated into English from the Marathi) by the Maharashtra Prantik Hindu Sabha in 1964. Unless otherwise specified, all subsequent quotations and page references are from the English translation in this edition (Savarkar 1964).

9. 'The word Sindhu in Sanskrit does not only mean the Indus but also the sea—*samudrarashna* which girdles the southern peninsula—so that this one word sindhu points out almost all the frontiers of our land at a single stroke.' (Savarkar 1964:20.)

10. Unlike in the case of *pitrabhoo* and *matrabhoo*, Savarkar seems to have used some interpretive licence here (and this is unlikely to be a matter of translation) for he uses the word 'blood' to mean *jati*, usually translated as caste. His argument is that 'Hindus' are all of one caste

and (therefore) of one blood because of the frequency of anuloma and pratiloma (i.e., inter-caste) marriages over the centuries and even millennia. It is interesting to compare Savarkar's criteria with Schneider's comments on the parallels between kinship by blood and marriage vs. nationality by birth and naturalization (Schneider 1976:215-6).

11. This eagerness to include what are now called 'Non-Resident' Indians has been a continuous feature of the Hindu right and specially the Vishwa Hindu Parishad. (See, for example, Van der Veer 1996:126.)

12. G. Balachandran (1996:116, citing Embree 1989:16). Balachandran goes on to comment: 'Thus the "Bharat of the Brahmanical ideology" was not only "made congruent" ... with the "India of the West's imagination", but also with the actual boundaries established at the end of Britain's nineteenth century conquest of the subcontinent'. (Balachandran 1996:16.)

13. For example, Dumont (1980), Chandra (1984:47ff.), etc.

14. Chatterjee 1986:141-43, see also note 31 (the quote from Nehru is from (Nehru 1946:387) and appears on p.141 of Chatterjee 1986).

15. For suggestive discussions of this crucial episode in the cultural-politics of contemporary India, see Rajadhyaksha (1990) and Rajagopal (1993).

16. The leaders of hindutva have themselves acknowledged the help provided by the religious teleserials of the 1980s (Rajagopal 1994).

17. Apart from my own inquiries, I have relied on the following documentary sources: People's Democratic Forum 1994, Kulkarni 1994 and Karnataka High Court 1992. I am indebted to Dr Sanjeev Kulkarni in Dharwad, Ms Chandrika Naik of the *Indian Express*, Hubli, and Ms Sudha Sitaraman of the PDF, Bangalore, who (besides providing access to the documentary sources cited above) gave generously of their time and expertise in helping to deepen my understanding of the issue. Of course, none of these people should be blamed for my views and interpretations.

18. Long after this description was written, I discovered to my amazement that I had failed to mention a large, much-frequented Sai Baba temple

sandwiched between the municipal courts and office of the Assistant Commissioner of Police. While this oversight surely indicates my own biases, it also reinforces the general point that even such undeniably physical realities as buildings and landscapes are located (and therefore seen or not seen in particular ways) within a socially conditioned field of vision.

19. Thus, for example, Ratna Naidu describes her experience of going to Bidar for fieldwork shortly after a communal riot there: 'The symbols of culture associated with an ethnic enemy evoke in us a psychic event ... rather than realistic recognition. I recall the uncanny fear which I experienced when the bus speeding me to field-work (in Bidar) suddenly took a turn to reveal a skyline studded with the beautiful domes of Islamic culture ... Later introspection made me realise that the absurd fear was that of a Hindu (even educated and cosmopolitan), on the eve of close interaction with an isolated *Muslim* dominated small town. I have tried to analyze the fear and am certain that it was an instinctive reaction to the architectural character of the city skyline.' (Naidu 1980:149, emphasis original.) And in his study of the growth of communalism in rural Marathwada, Thomas Blom Hansen reports on the Shiv Sena-led unemployed youth of large semi-urban villages agitating against Muslim encroachments on public space; the explicit aims of the Sena are to 'scale down the "undue visibility" of the Muslims, and it wanted, plain and simple, the business opportunities at the bus-stand for the Hindu youth.' This is amplified by an on-the-spot conversation with a respondent who points out to Hansen the visual offensiveness of Muslim structures. (Hansen 1996:192.)

20. In this connection, it may be useful to examine the vernacular vocabularies of territoriality which have accompanied urban communalism. The English words 'area' and 'society' or 'colony' (from housing society/colony), for example, seem to have joined older terms like mohalla, para, gali, chawl, ilaka, oni, and so on.

21. It has to be remembered, however, that the Shiv Sena did not embark upon its political career as a specifically *communal* organization, but

acquired/claimed this identity only in the late 1980s and specially the '90s. Also, the initial spread of the organization was more haphazard than planned, as admitted by Thackeray himself (Gupta 1982:72-74). But by following its 'natural' trajectory, the Sena found itself concentrated in certain kinds of neighbourhoods and among certain types of families. As Gerard Heuze notes: 'Within the *shakhas*, posts of responsibility are very often entrusted to a group of brothers, or brothers and uncle, sometimes sons and father. The *shakha* being considered as a new family, or as an extension of the family, is thus not just a simple metaphor.' (Heuze 1995:218.) While this is hardly atypical of other Indian political organizations, the important difference is that in the Shiv Sena this is explicitly encouraged and defended as 'perfectly natural and positive'.

22. See Dipankar Gupta (1982:75-80, 89-90). The Sena has, of course, borrowed this overall strategy from the Rashtriya Swayamsevak Sangh (RSS) which first pioneered it. As is well known, the traditional habitats of the RSS and the social geography of the urban middle and lower-middle classes are closely intertwined (Basu et al. 1993). And as Tanika Sarkar (in her valuable study of the Rashtra Sevika Samiti) has found, the women's wing of the RSS places even more emphasis than its male counterpart on low-key but unrelenting ideological work in the immediate social vicinity of its cadres: the intimate and intensely particular spaces of domesticity and the family (Sarkar 1991).

23. Kalpana Sharma, a Bombay-based journalist, notes that the maha-arti was launched on 11 December (during a lull in the communal disturbances following 2 December), in a temple (Gol Deval) strategically located between Muslim-dominated and Sena-BJP dominated localities. As she points out: 'A *maha-arti* is not an everyday Hindu ritual and even when one is held, it does not take place on the street outside a temple. Yet the Shiv Sena decided to make an issue of the fact that the Muslims have to spill out on the street during prayers on Friday because their mosques are too small to accommodate the entire congregation. Their leadership was quoted as saying that this

would help "recapture the streets for Hindus and end the policy of appeasement of the Muslim minority"'. (Sharma 1995:278.)

24. Such instances have been reported in several major communal riots, but a recent (and relatively well-documented) instance is once again in Bombay. Evidence for this emerged in the hearings of the Sri Krishna Commission, specially during the examination of the notorious Shiv Sena MLA (now an MP), Madhukar Sarpotdar. (The hearings were being reported by the daily press, but extensive accounts can also be found in the fortnightly *Frontline*.) Sadly, fresh evidence of this sort is being provided regularly—the Gujarat riots of March–April 2002 offer yet another (and possibly the most sustained) instance of systematically organized communal violence.

25. Detailed accounts of such instances are to be found in Veena Das's attempts to explore the spatialization of violence in the anti-Sikh riots of Delhi following Indira Gandhi's assassination in 1984, and in the study of the Khurja riots. (Das 1996, Chakravarti et al. 1992.)

26. Despite their regulation, loudspeakers are used to hurl abusive and insulting slogans, and to whip up mass hysteria. (In the 1984 Ganesh procession, the police confiscated 300 unlicenced public address systems.) The Bonalu procession, in which men now outnumber women, has resulted in major riots in 1981 (the first time it was reorganized on the model of the 1980 Ganesh procession), and 1984. The Ganesh procession has provoked at least half a dozen riots since 1980.

27. To begin with, Naidu reveals that some of the investigators in her study, 'who are old city residents and participate in the Ganesh procession, say that they always carry a knife during the procession—a telling commentary on what the culture of religious processions has deteriorated into'. (Naidu 1990:134.)

28. This, of course, is not an exceptional event, since the cow has often served as a symbolic rallying point in Hindu-Muslim conflict in the subcontinent. See, for example, Yang (1980) and Freitag (1980).

5. Caste Inequalities in India Today

1. I have pursued this theme in greater detail in two academic papers, one focusing on the factors of disciplinary location responsible for the lopsided understanding of caste in Indian sociology, and the other suggesting what sociologists need to do to re-orient social policy relating to caste inequality. (Deshpande 2003a , 2003b.)

2. It is important to emphasize that this is a general assessment of the discipline as a whole – although some scholars have indeed written on the material inequality aspect of caste (André Béteille and Gerald Berreman are the best known examples; for examples, see Béteille 1991a, 1991b, and Berreman 1979), they have been the exceptions that prove the rule of disciplinary indifference. 'Explanations for so massive and so obvious an error of omission must necessarily be complex,' as Satish Saberwal (1999:106) has written in an important article discussing the invisibility in Indian sociology of what he calls 'secular inequalities', meaning thereby a more general conception of inequality than merely caste inequality (such as the unequal income distribution and high levels of poverty and so on). His explanation is in terms of the prevailing state/national ideologies, the influence of American cultural anthropology and the personal backgrounds of Indian sociologists. It is interesting to note, however, that Saberwal's article (first published in 1979) is itself almost 'invisible' in the literature. Although it has been included in an anthology on social inequality in India (Sharma 1999), it is not discussed or cited in the mainstream literature, including, for example, Béteille (1991c), or three major anthologies on caste published recently (Sharma and Chatterjee 1994; M.N. Srinivas 1996b; and Fuller 1996).

3. Sociologists have been struggling with these implications of received models of caste for a long time. A comprehensive critique of these issues (and of the Dumont model in particular) is to be found in Dipankar Gupta's essay on 'Continuous hierarchies and discrete castes' (Gupta 2000).

4. In his critique of Dumont and Leach, André Béteille has argued that

conceptualizing castes as non-antagonistic and complementary strata deflects attention from conflict and competition among them. ('The politics of "non-antagonistic" strata,' in Béteille 1991.)

5. As A.M. Shah (1999:199-200) has pointed out, studies of what Srinivas has called the 'horizontal dimension' of caste went into a decline after 1931, the last effective census to report caste. Their place was taken in independent India by the 'village studies' tradition of scholarship, so that the 'vertical' unity of caste(s) received much greater attention than their 'horizontal' unity. This is the background to the dearth of macro data on caste inequality so sharply highlighted by the Mandal controversy.

6. Partial exceptions are to be found in Shri Prakash, 1997, and Radhakrishnan, 1996.

7. For a critique of the main arguments cited to oppose inclusion of caste in the Census, see Deshpande 1999.

8. The problems have to do with changes in the 'reference period' for the 55th Round survey (the period over which respondents are asked to report their consumption of various commodities). It is feared that these changes may make the 55th Round data incompatible with the previous rounds, so that comparisons across time cannot be made reliably. However, I am not comparing across rounds but across caste/community groups within the same round, and there is no reason to believe that different castes/communities will be differently affected by the changes in the reference period.

9. I must emphasize that these are only rough guesses because the NSSO does not publish data on cross-tabulations of caste with community – that is, it does not tell us how many sample households were both Christian *and* Scheduled Tribe, OBC *and* Muslim etc. So, when we devise an estimate of 'Hindu Upper Castes' by subtracting the non-Hindu religions from the 'Other Castes' category, we are bound to get an underestimate because of the 'double subtraction' of those households that belong to SC, ST, or OBC *as well as* a non-Hindu religious community. However, this is unlikely to make a huge difference to *comparative proportions* because Muslims are the

only sizeable minority, and within them, it is the OBC Muslims who are probably the most numerous. Nevertheless, it is important for the reader to realize that the 'Hindu Upper Caste' estimates are provided only for illustrative purposes and must not be treated on a par with the other figures. That is why the Tables including it bear a question mark.

10. But perhaps the problem would persist even if these technical issues were not involved, for, as social scientists all over the world know only too well, it is much more difficult to study the rich and powerful than it is to study the poor and powerless. Unlike 'normal' subjects of research, people of higher economic and social status than the researcher are usually able to simply deny access or, at the very least, to shape the conditions and results of research.

11. See the letter from S.S. Gill, Secretary of the Commission, requesting this information reproduced in Appendix VII of the Mandal Commission Report.

6. *The Centrality of the Middle Class*

1. 'As has been frequently remarked and bemoaned, Marx never systematically defined and elaborated the concept of class, in spite of the centrality of that concept to his work. To the perpetual frustration of people who seek in the texts of Marx authoritative answers to theoretical problems, in the one place where he promises such an elaboration—the final chapter of *Capital* Volume 3, entitled 'Classes'—the text stops after only a page.' Erik Olin Wright (1985:6).

2. There were actually three 'fundamental classes' identified in the plan for *Capital*, namely the working class, capitalists and landlords. The last category has spawned a separate literature on the development of capitalism in agriculture.

3. For example, the recent writings of Pavan Varma, Sumanta Banerjee, or Partha Chatterjee.

4. Barbara Ehrenreich shows how some of the best known works in

American sociology in recent decades have unselfconsciously located themselves in this class (Ehrenreich 1989:3-5).

5. See Deepak Lal, Rakesh Mohan and I. Natarajan (2001) for an interesting comparison of the NSSO and MISH.

6. As Stuart Hall notes, the linkages effected through articulation are conceived as socially constructed and therefore open to re-construction; as maintaining the distinctness of the entities linked while at the same time enabling them to function in tandem; and as the object of political struggles in the process of building hegemony (Hall 1985:113-14, n.2).

7. The point is not that such work is inapplicable to India because it is simply 'Western' in some essential sense, but that it is unable to address the *specificities* of the Indian context. For example, it is well known that Bourdieu developed his notion of symbolic capital as an ethnographer of Algeria. But Bourdieu's important work—while acknowledging symbolic capital to be a crucial form of property—treats it as a characteristic feature of a *pre-capitalist* social system, thereby implying its irrelevance for a capitalist society. On the other hand, his development of this notion through his (later) ethnographic work on French society, where cultural capital is recognized as producing 'distinction' in a contemporary capitalist setting, is overly aestheticized and distanced from the operations of the economy, so that its property-like aspects are underplayed. This obviously requires a much fuller discussion which I cannot enter into here.

8. A more detailed discussion of this issue is to be found in Deshpande 1996b.

9. It is in this sense that both the small town clerical worker as well as the metropolitan fashion photographer are members of the same class, despite all the obvious differences between them. For a different perspective on this problem, see the debate between Rudra (1989) and his critics (Iyer 1989a, 1989b; Béteille 1989; and Bardhan 1989).

10. The term is used here in its straightforward Gramscian sense of political domination based more on consent than overt coercion, achieved by a coalitional group that has been ideologically knitted

into a relatively cohesive bloc.

11. Arnold's well-known projection of a slide towards 'anarchy' which the upper classes ('barbarians'), the working classes ('populace'), and even most members of the middle-trading classes ('philistines') are unable to prevent, ends by vesting hope in a small minority from among the middle classes (and perhaps enlightened members of the others as well) who will stand up for 'culture' (Arnold 1960).

12. Estimated by mapping 55th Round NSSO computed proportion on to 1991 Census data. See Ch. 5 for details.

13. But see also Partha Chatterjee's (1997) critique of this position.

14. I borrow this formulation from Gayatri Spivak, who has used it in another context to demonstrate the problems associated with the vexed question: 'Can the Subaltern Speak?' (Spivak 1988).

7. *Globalization and the Geography of Cultural Regions*

1. As we saw in Chapter 2, 'modernization' had a similar career in the 1960s and '70s , when it was used indiscriminately to refer to a wide range of processes and phenomena.

2. I am not entering into a detailed review of the literature here; the best known early works include Featherstone (ed.) 1990, Friedman 1990, Robertson 1992, Hannerz 1996, and Appadurai 1997. Since then there has been a flood of books, specially edited volumes, on the subject.

3. Although the more careful commentators are very aware of this problem, this has not prevented the concept of globalization from being thought of in general terms as 'increasing long-distance interconnectedness, at least across national boundaries, preferably between continents as well' (Hannerz 1996:17).

4. For a recent discussion of this specific issue, see Samina Mishra's account of cable operators in the south Delhi neighbourhood of Lajpat Nagar (Mishra 1999).

5. In the 1981 Census study on regional divisions which extended to

the sub-district level for the first time, Uttara Kannada is placed in a different regional classification at the broadest (first digit) level itself; though the remaining three districts are in the same first and second level classifications, the third digit level places Dharwad on the one hand and Bijapur and Belgaum on the other in different regions. See Census 1981, *Regional Divisions of India: A Cartographic Analysis*, Occasional Papers, Series I, Volume IX, Karnataka, specially the map on p. 29.

6. The logic for this definition of the family does not rest in the structure of kinship networks but rather in the practical consideration of the information respondents are likely to be able to provide with reasonable accuracy. Since it is unlikely that most respondents will know much about their grandparents' first cousins, the first generation has been limited to siblings, thus making for an asymmetry. Moreover, 'ego' is defined as a mature adult because we need persons who have gone through most stages of the life cycle in order to generate information about spatial spread—children, for example, will yield much less data.

7. The only exception is one member of G2, who was a doctor in the Indian National Army of Subhas Chandra Bose and served in Singapore and Myanmar.

8. There is no obvious reason for this striking difference: both Lingayat families are very well off (one of them is actually quite wealthy) and reasonably well educated, nor are they (today) land-based families that can be expected to spread less.

9. It is possible that this cell too could contain a non-zero value after an unconfirmed response is confirmed.

10. As an example, one can cite a well-known series of advertisements for the Tata group of companies which compared places and things Indian to their global counterparts: Bombay was compared to Beijing or New York, an Indian steel plant was compared to a German one, and so on. This is the opposite of the essentialization that is an integral part of the spatial strategy of hindutva.

11. For an overview of this literature, see Harvey (1989), specially Part II, Chs. 7-11, 'The political-economic transformation of late

twentieth century capitalism.'
12. For a rich variety of perspectives on this set of issues, see the articles in the volume edited by Mike Featherstone (1990), specially those by Robertson, Wallerstein, Smith, Arnason, Hannerz, Appadurai, and Beyer.

Bibliography

Ahmad, Aijaz 1996: 'Class, Nation and State: Intermediate Classes in Peripheral Societies,' in Aijaz Ahmad, *Lineages of the Present: Political Essays*, Tulika, New Delhi, pp. 44-72.

Anderson, Benedict 1983: *Imagined Communities*, Verso, London.

Anderson, Benedict 1991: *Imagined Communities*, 2nd edition, Verso, London.

Appadurai, Arjun 1997: *Modernity at Large: Cultural Dimensions of Globalization*, Oxford University Press, Delhi.

Appadurai, Arjun and Carol Breckenridge 1996: 'Public Modernity in India,' in C. Breckenridge (ed.) *Consuming Modernity: Public Culture in Contemporary India*, Oxford University Press, Delhi, pp. 1-20.

Arnold, Matthew 1960 [1869]: *Culture and Anarchy*, J. Dover Wilson (ed.), paperback edition, Cambridge University Press, Cambridge.

Balachandran, G. 1996: 'Religion and Nationalism in Modern India,' in Basu, Kaushik and Sanjay Subrahmanyam (ed.), *Unravelling the Nation: Sectarian Conflict and India's Secular Identity*, Penguin Books, New Delhi, pp. 81-128.

Banerjee, Sumanta 1989: *The Parlour and the Streets: Elite and Popular Culture in Nineteenth Century Bengal*, Seagull Books, Calcutta.

Banuri, Tariq 1990: 'Development and the Politics of Knowledge: A Critical Interpretation of the Social Role of Modernization;' and 'Modernization and its Discontents: A Cultural Perspective on Theories of Development,' in Stephen Marglin and Frederique Apfel Marglin (eds.) *Dominating Knowledge: Development, Culture and Resistance*, Clarendon Press, Oxford, pp. 29-101.

Bardhan, Pranab 1989: 'The Third Dominant Class,' in *Economic and Political Weekly*, v.24, n.3, 21 January, pp. 155-56.

Basu, Kaushik and Sanjay Subrahmanyam (ed.) 1996: *Unravelling the Nation: Sectarian Conflict and India's Secular Identity*, Penguin Books, New Delhi.

Basu, Tapan, Pradip Datta, Sumit Sarkar, Tanika Sarkar, Sambuddha Sen 1993: *Khaki Shorts Saffron Flags*, Tracts for the Times, n.1, Orient Longman, New Delhi.

Bendix, Reinhard 1967: 'Tradition and Modernity Reconsidered,' *Comparative Studies in Society and History.* v.9. (April), pp. 292-346.

Berreman, Gerald 1979: *Caste and Other Inequities: Essays on Inequality*, Folklore Institute, Meerut.

Béteille, André 1989: 'Are the Intelligentsia a Ruling Class?' in *Economic and Political Weekly*, v.24, n.3, 21 January, pp.151-55.

Béteille, André 1991a: 'Distributive Justice and Institutional Well-Being,' in *Economic and Political Weekly*, Annual Number, v.26, nos.11-12, March.

Béteille, André 1991b: 'The Reproduction of Inequality: Occupation, Caste and Family,' in *Contributions to Indian Sociology*, n.s., v.25, n.1, Jan-Jun 1991.

Béteille, André 1991c: *Society and Politics in India*, Oxford University Press, Delhi.

Beyer, Peter F. 1990: 'Privatization and the Public Influence of Religion in Global Society,' in Featherstone (1990), pp. 373-396.

Black, Cyril E. 1966: *The Dynamics of Modernization: A Study in Comparative History,* Harper and Row, New York.

Bourdieu, Pierre 1984: *Distinction: A Social Critique of the Judgement of Taste*, tr. Richard Nice, Harvard University Press, Cambridge, Massachusetts.

Burghart, Richard 1990: 'Ethnographers and Their Local Counterparts in India,' in R. Fardon (ed.) *Localizing Strategies: Regional Traditions of Ethnographic Writings,* Scottish Academic Press, Edinburgh, pp. 260-78.

Chakravarti, Uma, Prem Chowdhury, Pradip Dutta, Zoya Hasan, Kumkum Sangari and Tanika Sarkar 1992: 'Khurja Riots 1990-91: Understanding the Conjuncture,' *Economic and Political Weekly* 27(18):951-965.

Chandra, Bipan 1984: *Communalism in Modern India*, Vikas, New Delhi.

Chandra, Bipan, 1966: *The Rise and Growth of Economic Nationalism in India*, People's Publishing House, New Delhi.

Chatterjee, Partha 1986: *Nationalist Thought and the Colonial World: A Derivative Discourse*, Zed Books, London.

Chatterjee, Partha 1994: *The Nation and its Fragments: Colonial and Postcolonial Histories*, Oxford University Press, Delhi.

Chatterjee, Partha 1997: 'Beyond the Nation? Or Within?,' *Economic and Political Weekly*, v.XXXII, nos.1-2, 4-11 January, pp. 30-34.

Clifford, James 1986: 'Introduction: Partial Truths,' in J. Clifford and G.E. Marcus (eds.) *Writing Culture: The Poetics and Politics of Ethnography*, University of California Press, Berkeley, pp. 1-26.

Cohn, Bernard 1987: *An Anthropologist Among the Historians and Other Essays*, Oxford University Press, Delhi.

Das, Veena 1995: *Critical Events: An Anthropological Perspective on Contemporary India*, Oxford University Press, Delhi.

Das, Veena 1996: 'The Spatialization of Violence: Case Study of a Communal Riot,' in Basu, Kaushik and Sanjay Subrahmanyam (ed.), *Unravelling the Nation: Sectarian Conflict and India's Secular Identity*, Penguin Books, New Delhi, pp. 157-203.

Deshpande, Satish 1993: 'Imagined Economies: Styles of Nation Building in Twentieth Century India,' in *Journal of Arts and Ideas*, nos.25-26, December, pp. 5-35.

Deshpande, Satish 1994: 'The Crisis in Sociology: A Tired Discipline?' *Economic and Political Weekly*, v.XXIX, n.10, 5 March, pp. 575-6.

Deshpande, Satish 1996: 'The Current Impasse in the Language of Rights: A Note on Questions of Context,' *Economic and Political Weekly*, Review of Political Economy, vol. 33, no. 5, 31 January 1998, pp. PE-11-15.

Deshpande, Satish 1999: 'Caste and the Census,' in *Sociological Bulletin*, v.48, nos.1 & 2, March-September 1999, pp. 257-262.

Deshpande, Satish 2003a: 'Caste Inequality and Indian Sociology: Notes on Questions of Disciplinary Location,' in Maitrayee Chaudhuri (ed.), *Recasting Indian Sociology: The Changing Contours of the Discipline*, Orient Longman, New Delhi, in press.

Deshpande, Satish 2003b: 'Confronting Caste Inequality: What Sociologists Must Do to Reorient Social Policy,' in S.M. Dahiwale (ed.), *Understanding Indian Society: Perspectives From Below*, forthcoming.

Dhareshwar, Vivek 1995a: '"Our Time": History, Sovereignty and Politics,' *Economic and Political Weekly.* v.30. n.6, pp. 317-24.

Dhareshwar, Vivek 1995b: 'Postcolonial in the Postmodern; or the Political After Modernity,' *Economic and Political Weekly,* (Review of Political Economy) v.30. n.30. pp. PE104-PE112.

Dumont, Louis [1964] 1980: 'Communalism and Nationalism,' in *Homo Hierarchicus*, Revised English edition, University of Chicago Press, Chicago, Appendix D, pp. 314-335.

Dumont, Louis 1964: 'Introductory Note: Change, Interaction and Comparison,' *Contributions to Indian Sociology* VII, (old series), (March), pp. 7-17.

Ehrenreich, Barbara 1989: *Fear of Falling: The Inner Life of the Middle Class*, Harper Perennial, New York.

Embree, Ainslee T. 1989: *Imagining India: Essays on Indian History*, Delhi.

Fabian, Johannes 1983: *Time and the Other: How Anthropology Makes its Object*, Columbia University Press, New York.

Featherstone, Mike (ed.) 1990: *Global Culture: Nationalism, Globalization and Modernity*, Sage Publications, New Delhi.

Freitag, Sandria 1980: 'Sacred Symbol as Mobilizing Ideology: The North Indian Search for a "Hindu" community,' in *Comparative Studies in Society and History*, v.22, n.4, October, pp. 597-625.

Friedman, Jonathan 1990: 'Being in the World: Globalization and Localization,' in Mike Featherstone, (ed.), *Global Culture: Nationalism, Globalization and Modernity*, Sage Publications, New Delhi.

Fuller, C.J. (ed.) 1996: *Caste Today*, Oxford University Press.

Gendzier, Irene 1985: *Managing Political Change: Social Scientists and the Third World*, Boulder, Westview Press, Colorado.

Gopal, Sarvepalli 1980: 'The Emergence of Modern Nationalism: Some Theoretical Problems in the Nineteenth and Early Twentieth Centuries,' in *Sociological Theories: Race and Colonialism*, UNESCO, Paris.

Gouldner, Alvin 1979: *The Future of Intellectuals and the Rise of the New Class*, Oxford University Press, New York.

Goyal, Santosh 1992a: 'Social Background of Officers of the Indian

Administrative Service', Appendix II, in Francine Frankel and M.S.A. Rao (eds.), *Dominance and State Power in Modern India: Decline of a Social Order*, v.1, Oxford University Press, Delhi.

Goyal, Santosh 1992b: 'Social Background of Top Corporate Officials in the Private and Public Sectors,' Appendix IV, in Francine Frankel and M.S.A. Rao (eds.), *Dominance and State Power in Modern India: Decline of a Social Order*, v.2, Oxford University Press, Delhi.

Guha, Ranajit (ed.) 1982: *Subaltern Studies I: Writings on South Asian History and Society.* Oxford University Press, Delhi.

Gupta, Dipankar 1982: *Nativism in a Metropolis: Shiv Sena in Bombay*, Manohar, Delhi.

Gupta, Dipankar 2000: *Interrogating Caste: Understanding Hierarchy and Difference in Indian Society*, Penguin Books, New Delhi.

Gupta, Dipankar 2001: *Culture, Space and the Nation-State*, Sage Publications, New Delhi

Hall, Stuart 1985: 'Signification, Representation, Ideology: Althusser and the Post-Structuralist Debates,' in *Critical Studies in Mass Communication*, v.2, n.2, June, pp. 91-114.

Hannerz, Ulf 1996: *Transnational Connections: Culture, People, Places*, Routledge, London and New York.

Hansen, Thomas Blom 1996: 'The Vernacularisation of Hindutva: The BJP and Shiv Sena in Rural Maharashtra,' in *Contributions to Indian Sociology*, v.30, n.2, July-December, pp. 177-214.

Harvey, David 1989: *The Postmodern Condition*, Blackwell, Oxford.

Hawthorn, Geoffrey 1987: *Enlightenment and Despair: A History of Social Theory.* (2nd edition), Cambridge University Press, Cambridge (UK).

Heuze, Gerard 1995: 'Cultural Populism: The Appeal of the Shiv Sena,' in Patel and Thorner (ed.), pp. 223-47.

Inkeles, Alex and David H. Smith 1974: *Becoming Modern: Individual Change in Six Developing Countries.* Heinemann, London.

Ishwaran, K. 1968: *Shivapur: A South Indian Village*, Routledge and Kegan Paul, London.

Iyer, Ramaswamy R. 1989a: 'Intelligentsia as a Ruling Class: Some Questions,' in *Economic and Political Weekly*, v.24, n.10, 11 March, pp.

529-32.

Iyer, Ramaswamy R. 1989b: 'Intelligentsia as a Ruling Class: An Alternative Hypothesis,' in *Economic and Political Weekly*, v.24, n.51, 23-30 December, pp. 2859-60.

John, Mary and Janaki Nair (eds.) 1998: *A Question of Silence? The Sexual Economies of Modern India,* Kali for Women, New Delhi.

Kapur, Geeta 1991: 'Place of the Modern in Indian Cultural Practice,' *Economic and Political Weekly.* v.26. n.49, pp. 2803-6.

Karnataka High Court 1992: Judgement delivered by Justice R.V. Vasanthakumar, in the Regular Second Appeal Nos.754/82 C/W.1 of 1983, between Anjuman-e-Islam, Hubli, and the Karnatak Board of Wakfs (Appellants); and B.S. Shettar and 92 others, Hubli-Dharwad Municipal Corporation, and State of Karnataka (Respondents). Judgement delivered 18 June, 1992.

Kaviraj, Sudipta 1988: 'A Critique of the Passive Revolution,' in *Economic and Political Weekly*, Special Number, v.23, n.27, November, pp. 2429-2443.

Kaviraj, Sudipta 1990: 'Capitalism and the Cultural Process,' in *Journal of Arts and Ideas*, n.19, May, pp. 61-72.

Kopf, David 1969: *British Orientalism and the Bengal Renaissance: The Dynamics of Indian Modernization, 1773-1835*, University of California Press, Berkeley.

Kulkarni, Sanjeev 1994: *Idga Maidandalli Dhwajarohanada Vivada: Ondu Vishleshane* (Flag Hoisting Controversy at Idgah Maidan: An Analysis), Janatantra Samaj (Citizens for Democracy), Dharwad, August (in Kannada).

Lal, Deepak, Rakesh Mohan and I. Natarajan 2002: 'Economic Reforms and Poverty Alleviation: A Tale of Two Surveys,' in *Economic and Political Weekly*, V.XXXVI, n.12, 24 March, pp. 1017-28.

Lefebvre, Henri 1991: *The Production of Space*, tr. D. Nicholson-Smith, Blackwell, Oxford.

Lerner, Daniel 1958: *The Passing of Traditional Society: Modernizing the Middle East*, Free Press, Glencoe (Illinois).

Lima Cruz, Maria Augusta 1998: 'Notes on Portuguese Relations with

Vijayanagara, 1500-1565,' in Sanjay Subrahmanyam (ed.), *Sinners and Saints: The Successors of Vasco da Gama*, Oxford University Press, Delhi.

Madan, T.N. 1995: *Pathways: Approaches to the Study of Society in India*, Oxford University Press, Delhi.

Madon, Justice D.P. 1974: *Report of the Commission of Inquiry into the Communal Disturbances at Bhiwandi, Jalgaon and Mahad in May 1970*, vols.I-VII, Home Department (Special), Government of Maharashtra.

Mandelbaum, David 1970: *Society in India* (2 vols), University of California Press, Berkeley.

Mayo Katherine 1927: *Mother India*, Jonathan Cape, London.

Mishra, Samina 1999: 'Dish is Life: Cable Operators and the Neighbourhood,' in Christiane Brosius and Melissa Butcher, (eds.), *Image Journeys: Audio-Visual Media and Cultural Change in India*, Sage Publications, New Delhi.

Misra, B.B. 1960: *The Indian Middle Classes: Their Growth in Modern Times*, Oxford University Press, Delhi.

Mukerji, Dhurjati Prasad 1955: 'Indian Tradition and Social Change,' (Presidential address to the first meeting of the Indian Sociological Society), in T.K. Oommen and Partha Mukherji (eds.) *Indian Sociology: Reflections and Introspections*, Popular Prakashan, Bombay, 1988, pp. 1-15.

Mukerji, Dhurjati Prasad 1948: *Sociology of Indian Culture*, 2nd edition, reprinted (1978) by Rawat Publications, Jaipur.

Mukherjee, Ramakrishna 1979: *Sociology of Indian Sociology*, Allied Publishers, Bombay.

Myrdal, Gunnar 1970: *An Approach to the Asian Drama: Methodological and Theoretical*, Vintage Books, New York.

Naidu, Ratna 1980: *The Communal Edge to Plural Societies: India and Malaysia*, Institute of Economic Growth and Vikas Publishing House, Delhi.

Naidu, Ratna 1992: *Old Cities, New Predicaments*, Sage Publications, New Delhi.

Nairn, Tom 1981: 'The Modern Janus,' Ch.9 in *The Breakup of Britain*, 2nd edition, Verso, London.

Naoroji, Dadabhai 1962 [1901]: Poverty and Un-British Rule in India, Publications Division, Ministry of Information and Broadcasting,

Government of India, New Delhi.

Natarajan, I. (ed.): *India Market Demographics Report 1998*, National Council for Applied Economic Research, New Delhi.

Nehru, Jawaharlal [1936] 1985: *An Autobiography*, Centenary Edition, Oxford University Press, Delhi.

Nehru, Jawaharlal 1980: *An Anthology*, edited by S. Gopal, Oxford University Press, New Delhi.

Nehru, Jawaharlal [1946] 1981: *The Discovery of India*, John Day, New York.

Oommen, T.K. 1997: *Citizenship and National Identity*, Sage Publications, New Delhi.

Pandey, Gyanendra 1991: 'In Defence of the Fragment: Writing About Hindu-Muslim Riots in India Today,' in *Economic and Political Weekly*, Annual Number, vol.XXVI, nos.11-12, March, pp. 559-572.

Panini, M.N. 1996: 'The Political Economy of Caste,' in M.N. Srinivas (ed.) *Caste: Its Twentieth Century Avatar*, Viking Penguin, New Delhi.

Patel, Sujata and Alice Thorner (eds.) 1996: *Bombay: Metaphor for Modern India*, Oxford University Press, Bombay/Delhi.

Peirano, Mariza G.S. 1991: 'For a Sociology of India: Some Comments From Brazil,' *Contributions to Indian Sociology*, (n.s.). v.25. n.2. pp. 321-7.

People's Democratic Forum (PDF) 1994: *Flag Without Tears: A Report on the Hubli Idga Maidan Issue*, Bangalore, December.

Prakash, Shri 1997: 'Reservations Policy for Other Backward Classes: Problems and Perspectives,' in V.A. Pai Panandiker (ed.), *The Politics of Backwardness: Reservation Policy in India*, Konark Publishers, New Delhi.

Prasad, Madhav 1998a: *The Ideology of Hindi Cinema: A Historical Construction*, Oxford University Press, Delhi.

Prasad, Madhav 1998b: 'Back to the Present,' *Cultural Dynamics*, v.10. n.2 (July), pp. 123-131.

Radhakrishnan, P. 1996: 'Mandal Commission Report: A Sociological Critique,' in M.N.Srinivas (ed.), *Caste: Its Twentieth Century Avatar*, Viking Penguin, New Delhi.

Raj, K.N. 1997: 'Planning: Getting the Economy on Track,' in *India* (special supplement issued by *The Hindu* on the 50th anniversary of Independence), August, pp. 107-9.

Rajadhyaksha, Ashish 1990: 'Beaming Messages to the Nation,' in *Journal of Arts and Ideas*, n.19, May, pp. 33-52.

Rajadhyaksha, Ashish 1993: 'The Phalke Era: Conflict of Traditional Form and Modern Technology,' in Tejaswini Niranjana, P. Sudhir and Vivek Dhareshwar (eds.), *Interrogating Modernity: Culture and Colonialism in India*, Seagull Books, Calcutta, pp. 47-82.

Rajagopal, Arvind 1993: 'The Rise of National Programming: The Case of Indian Television,' in *Media, Culture, and Society*, January.

Rajagopal, Arvind 1994: 'Ram Janmabhoomi, Consumer Identity, and Image-Based Politics,' in *Economic and Political Weekly*, v.XXIX, n.27, 2 July, pp. 1659-1668.

Reddy, Justice Jaganmohan 1970: *Report: Inquiry into the Communal Disturbances at Ahmedabad and Other Places in Gujarat on and after 18th September 1969*, (Justice Jaganmohan Reddy Commission of Enquiry), Home Department, Government of Gujarat.

Robertson, Roland 1992: *Globalization: Social Theory and Global Culture*, Sage Publications, New Delhi.

Rosen, George 1985: *Western Economists and Eastern Societies: Agents of Change in South Asia, 1950-1970*, Oxford University Press, Delhi.

Rudolph, Lloyd I., and Susanne Hoeber Rudolph 1967: *The Modernity of Tradition: Political Development in India*, University of Chicago Press, Chicago.

Rudra, Ashok 1989: 'The Emergence of the Intelligentsia as a Ruling Class in India,' in *Economic and Political Weekly*, v.24, n.3, 21 January, pp. 142-150.

Saberwal, Satish 1986: 'Uncertain Transplants: Anthropology and Sociology in India,' in T.K. Oommen and Partha Mukherji (eds.), *Indian Sociology: Reflections and Introspections*, Popular Prakashan, Bombay, 1986, pp. 214-232.

Saberwal, Satish 1999: 'Sociologists and Inequality,' in K.L. Sharma (ed.) *Social Inequality in India* (Originally in *Economic and Political Weekly*, Annual Number 1979).

Sack, Robert David 1986: *Human Territoriality: Its Theory and History*, Cambridge University Press, Cambridge.

Said, Edward 1993: *Culture and Imperialism*, Alfred Knopf, New York.

Saran, A.K. 1958: 'India,' in J.S. Roucek (ed.). *Contemporary Sociology*, Philosophical Library, New York, pp. 1013-34.

Sarkar, Sumit 1973: *The Swadeshi Movement in Bengal*, People's Publishing House, Delhi.

Sarkar, Tanika 1991: 'Woman as Communal Subject: Rashtrasevika Samiti and Ram Janmabhoomi Movement,' in *Economic and Political Weekly*, v.26, n.35, 31 August.

Savarkar, V.D. 1964: *Samagra Savarkar Wangmaya*, v.6, Maharashtra Prantik Hindu Sabha, Poona.

Schneider, David 1976: 'Notes Towards a Theory of Culture,' in Basso, K. and H. Selby, *Meaning in Anthropology*, Univ. of New Mexico Press.

Searle-Chatterjee, Mary and Ursula Sharma (eds.) 1994: *Contextualizing Caste: Post- Dumontian Approaches*, Blackwell Publishers/The Sociological Review, Oxford.

Sen, Abhijit 2000: 'Estimates of Consumer Expenditure and its Distribution: Priorities after NSS 55th Round,' *Economic and Political Weekly*, v.XXXV, n.51, 16 December, 2000.

Shah, A.M. 1999: 'Division and Hierarchy: An Overview of Caste in Gujarat,' in K.L. Sharma (ed.) *Social Inequality in India*, pp. 199-234.

Shah, Mihir 1985: 'The Kaniatchi Form of Labour,' *Economic and Political Weekly*, (Review of Political Economy), v.20. n.30. pp. PE65-PE78.

Sharma, K.L. (ed.) 1999: *Social Inequality in India*, (revised 2nd edition), Rawat, Jaipur and New Delhi.

Sharma, Kalpana 1995: 'Chronicle of a Riot Foretold,' in Patel and Thorner (eds.), pp. 268-86.

Singer, Milton (ed.) 1975: *Traditional India: Structure and Change*, Rawat, Jaipur.

Singer, Milton 1972: *When A Great Tradition Modernizes: An Anthropological Approach to Indian Civilization*, Praeger, New York.

Smith, Anthony D. 1986: *The Ethnic Origins of Nations*, Blackwell, Oxford.

Soja, Edward 1989: *Postmodern Geographies: The Reassertion of Space in Social Theory*, Verso, London.

Spivak, Gayatri Chakravorty 1988: 'Can the Subaltern Speak?' in Cary

Nelson and Lawrence Grossberg (eds.), *Marxism and the Interpretation of Culture*, Univ. of Illinois Press, Urbana and Chicago, pp. 271-313.

Srinivas, M.N. 1971a: *Social Change in Modern India*, University of California Press, Berkeley (First published 1966, fifth printing).

Srinivas, M.N. 1971b: 'Modernization: A Few Queries,' in A.R. Desai (ed.), *Essays on Modernization of Underdeveloped Societies,* Thacker & Co., Bombay, v.1. pp. 149-58.

Srinivas, M.N., 1992: 'Studying One's Own Culture: Some Thoughts,' in M.N. Srinivas, *On Living in a Revolution and Other Essays*, Oxford University Press, Delhi.

Srinivas, M.N. 1996a: *Indian Society Through Personal Writings*, Oxford University Press, Delhi

Srinivas, M.N. (ed.) 1996b: *Caste: Its Twentieth Century Avatar*, Viking Penguin, New Delhi.

Srinivas, M.N. and M.N. Panini 1973: 'The Development of Sociology and Social Anthropology in India,' in T. K. Oommen and Partha Mukherji (eds.) *Indian Sociology: Reflections and Introspections,* Popular Prakashan, Bombay, 1986, pp. 16-55.

Tandon, Prakash 1961: *Punjabi Century: 1857-1947*, University of California Press, Berkeley.

Tipps, Dean C. 1973: 'Modernization Theory and the Comparative Study of Societies: A Critical Perspective,' *Comparative Studies in Society and History*, v.15, (March), pp. 199-226.

Tuan, Yi-Fu 1977: *Space and Place: The Perspective of Experience*, University of Minnesota Press, Minneapolis.

Uberoi, Patricia (ed.) 1996: *Social Reform, Sexuality and the State*, Sage Publications, New Delhi.

van der Veer, Peter 1996: *Religious Nationalisms: Hindus and Muslims in India*, Oxford University Press, Delhi.

Vanaik, Achin 1993: *India: The Painful Transition*, Verso, London.

Vanaik, Achin 2002: 'Consumerism and New Classes in India,' Ch.14 in Sujata Patel, Jashodhara Bagchi and Krishna Raj (eds.), *Thinking Social Science in India: Essays in Honour of Alice Thorner*, Sage Publications, New Delhi, pp. 227-234.

Wallerstein, Immanuel and Etienne Balibar 1991: *Race, Nation, Class: Ambiguous Identities*, Verso, London.

Williams, Raymond 1983: *Keywords: A Vocabulary of Culture and Society*, (Revised edition), Oxford University Press, New York.

Williams, Raymond 1989: *The Politics of Modernism: Against the New Conformists*, Verso, London.

Wright, Erik Olin 1985: *Classes*, Verso, London.

Yang, Anand 1980: 'Sacred Symbol and Sacred Space in Rural India: Community Mobilization in the "Anti-Cow Killing" Riot of 1893,' in *Comparative Studies in Society and History*, v.22, n.4, October, pp. 576-96.

Index